I RODE THE

ROCK TRAIN

BRUCE E. NORRIS

Published by Hemingway Publishers

Cover design by Hemingway Publishers

ISBN: Printed in the United States

Dedication

This book is dedicated to Elaine, Brad, Angela and Margaret, for putting up with my stupid idling for as long as I can remember. Angelo, for early mentoring, friendship and always ready to help. Eric, Mike, T. Rise, Leonard, Willy, Aundre, John, Ken, Mark and everybody else who were in the bands that kept the rock-n-roll train steaming forward. Zack, Andrew, Billy, Tori and the rest of the crew that kept Klownz rolling down the tracks. And many thanks, a wink, and a smile to the club owners whose stages we made a complete mess of.

Other books by Bruce E. Norris

What Lurks Below

Escape Socotra Island…dead men still tell no tales

The Springs

Contact the author at brucenorrisbooks@aol.com

Visit Author Bruce E. Norris on Facebook and X

Visit fb @ Klownz Mock and Roll to watch Klownz videos

Visit YouTube to watch F videos

Foreword

Are you one of those people who believe you were put on this planet to achieve one thing and one thing only? Well, I was that person.

I was introduced to music in my pre-teens, just like everybody else I know. But when I became a teenager, things changed. I became a huge fan of rock-n-roll music and the bands that played it — not all bands, but the ones that really meant something to me. Bands like The Beatles, Rolling Stones, Kinks, KISS, Alice Cooper, Cheap Trick, Sweet, Slade, Ramones, and The Bay City Rollers. There's more, of course, but I don't want to make this book too thick.

These were the rock groups that got me going. I loved the music, the lifestyle, the look and the attitude they depicted. I liked it so much that I wanted to be a part of it. I had to jump aboard the Rock-N-Roll Train and ride the rails of my rock-roll fantasy.

You can say I was lucky or unlucky enough to be in rock bands F, The Remedy, Klownz, Easy Access and Slip Friction.

Being a member of all these bands took 31 years of my life. I guess I can easily compare it to being on another planet because I couldn't have cared less about what was going on in everyday life. I had tunnel vision, and I was on the Rock-N-Roll Train, speeding toward the light at the end of the tunnel where I would be a huge, successful rock star.

During these years of ups and downs, good and bad times, there were a few times when I'd had enough and tried to quit, only to realize there was nothing out there for me to replace it. Deep down, I knew there was no way I could survive and become a normal human being.

That being said, it was the year 2012 when I finally jumped off the train. That was the year my first book was published. Thanks to my son, I slipped and fell into becoming a published author.

I forgot to tell you that I have no boundaries. No walls or barriers that would keep an exemplary person down. If I wanted to do something or be somebody, I just did it as if I knew what I was doing. If I believed in it and worked hard enough, I believed the mysteries of the universe would catch up and make it happen.

That's how I jumped into a band without knowing how to play an instrument or how to become a published author. I did it by mimicking the people successfully doing it.

My son was reading a book to me in the backyard for his summer reading assignment. I laughed and asked him who couldn't write a book like the one he was reading. I read through pages without a period or comma, for crying out loud.

When he looked up at me, he said, "You can't, Dad," and it was game on. I was going to show my son that you could do anything you set your mind to do.

First, I read all the books from a well-known author so I could see how he kept it moving without boring the readers to death. After that, I set out to write my book.

It took me five years because I was winging it, but it felt easy. I pretended to be the well-known author and carried on. Words didn't have to rhyme like a song, and before I knew it, it was finished.

Since I had no barriers or brick walls to stop me, I believed I had the best book on planet Earth and had it published. No doubt, the feedback/response was good, and it sold all over the world, so I challenged myself to see if I could write another. When that became a success, too, I did a third, and its first week of release was more successful than the other two books put together! EUREKA! Now, I'm a published author with books selling all over the world! Pinch me; I must be dreaming.

The thing is, I was so engrossed in writing these books that I forgot that my life was meaningless if I wasn't in a rock group or writing songs. As I sit here writing this book, it's been 13 years since I needed that rock-n-roll lifeline. I'm cured!

Sometimes, more times than I want to admit, when my family and I go out to dinner or have a drink somewhere and there's a live band playing, I get the urge to start a band again. It's terrible; I feel like an addict.

Looking back now, I know I would have done some things differently. But I'll always remember the good times, bad times and completely bizarre times I had riding the Rock-N-Roll Train.

Sadly, most of the guys I played with no longer give me the time of day. I thought I was an agreeable guy with my bandmates, but I was probably a relentless hellion, focused on driving that train at full speed ahead to the end of the tracks.

Some of the bands we played with and musicians that I thought were close friends have had reunions and get-togethers that I was never invited to. It stings a little, but that's ok. It's only rock n roll, and I like it.

Table of Contents

All aboard, welcome to the Rock-N-Roll Train

My love affair with music started in 1973 when I was 10 years old. My best friend, named Patrick *(I will not write their last names to protect the guilty)*, and I were playing around in his front yard when his older brother, who was always in trouble with the law and had just gotten out of jail, came home with a new record. It was called *"Band on the Run"* by ex-Beatle Paul McCartney.

In the sixties, my age had a single digit, and music was the furthest thing from my mind, but I surely knew who the Beatles were. My idea of good music was the Monkees and Batman theme songs. Those were the two reasons we stopped playing outside to go inside the house to watch TV.

Patrick and I chose the new Paul McCartney and Wings album and listened to it. Remember, I wasn't into music yet, but everybody on the planet knew the Beatles. They were and still are the gods of rock-n-roll. Funny, it's been 55 years since their breakup, and there still isn't any other band to carry their torch.

At that time, and at my age, whenever I heard the word Beatles, it gave me the impression of something dark — the four of them with long hair and black clothes leading a generation of followers around. Whatever they said or did, their followers would do the same.

Listening to 'Band on the Run' was probably the first record I ever listened to from start to finish. Patrick was more into it than me, but I liked it. It didn't make me want to jump on the Rock-N-Roll Train, but it sure led me to the train station.

I Rode The Rock Train

By 1975, Patrick and I stopped hanging out together. Some bullies in the neighborhood seemed to want to kick his butt every time he stuck it out of the door, so he just decided not to play outside anymore. Wow, what a drag! But as I learned then and damn well know now, all good things come to an end.

To get my mind off the fact that my buddy didn't want to play outside anymore, I signed up to play on a Little League baseball team. While on the team, I met my new best friend, Jim. Jim and I quickly found out that he was a music nut; he even slept with the radio on.

Every weekend, we would sleep over at one or the other's house, usually in a tent in the backyard. I had no choice but to listen to all that cool music late at night while trying to sleep. This is when I really started getting into music.

One day, we were in the car going to the grocery store with his mom, squeezing each other's fingers with pliers until the tears started pouring out of one of us; I heard 2 songs that hit me like a bolt of lightning. It was the Who's "Pinball Wizard" and Elton John's "Philadelphia Freedom." Don't ask me why, but when they played those songs back-to-back, it struck a chord in me and changed my life forever. I wanted to get in on that action. I wanted to be a rock star!

One night, we had a sleepover in a tent in my backyard. We were running around the streets looking for the boogeyman, and he suddenly said, "At 11:00, we have to go back to the tent and watch Don Kirshner's Rock concert (or Midnight Special, I forgot which one). We were having so much fun, I couldn't believe the little candy-ass wanted to go in and watch television.

Reluctantly, I went back to the tent with him and turned on the little 10" black and white TV and watched the show. He told me there was this new band out that he had to see. Ok, whatever, I couldn't care less. Near the end of the show, his band finally came on. The band was like nothing I had ever seen before. Their one-of-a-kind, unique image blew my mind.

They came running out on stage with matching plaid uniforms and pants at least 2 feet higher from their ankles. They wore tartan scarves all over, and mostly, the female audience went wild as they sang their hit "Saturday Night."

Wow! I loved it! I became an instant fan, which was not too cool since most of their fans were girls. I didn't care if I was the only guy who thought they were great. They sounded good and had an image, something I believe wholeheartedly is a key ingredient that every band should have.

Even to this day, I will play a CD with my friends, and they think they sound great. The sound is pure and crisp. Funny thing, when I tell them it's the Bay City Rollers, they look up and say… "Who"? They didn't last long, but they sure left an impression for three years.

So, there I was, 12 years old, loving what I heard on the radio. I have family that lives in Belgium, and we used to visit about every 4 years.

In the summer of '76, we went over for a visit. I always thought my uncle over there was cool and knew a lot about music. He had a record collection and showed me some bands I'd never heard of. Bands that were huge in Europe and England but unheard of in America. To check out his reaction, I told him I was a Bay City Rollers fan. He didn't laugh his ass off like I thought he would because overseas at that time, the Bay City Rollers were as popular as the Beatles.

Nevertheless, he suggested a manlier group to look into. He reached into his enormous record collection, pulled out "T Rex Greatest Hits," and presented it to me with two hands and head bowed as if he were giving me the Holy Grail. I loved it then, and it's still one of my favorites! I played it so much that I think I wore out the grooves.

T Rex was another one of those groups that looked like Rock Stars instead of roadies. To this day, and after all I've been through, I still believe that dressing up to make your band stand out is half the attraction, which I confirmed to myself years later with my band 'Klownz.'

While in Belgium that summer, my uncle also got me hooked on Abba, Sweet, Slade and a gruff band called 'The Animals.' It was there that I also started collecting albums of the rock gods themselves, The Beatles.

1976 was also the year I became a lifelong fan of Alice Cooper and KISS. For the next few years, I rode my bike down to the record store and bought all kinds of records. Back then, it seemed that every time I turned around, Alice Cooper and KISS came out with a brand-new record; it was incredible. Back then, KISS made two albums a year. I remember going to the store to get my copy of 'Destroyer,' standing in stunned silence, holding a copy of 'Rock-N-Roll Over." In just eight months' time, KISS came out with another full-length album!

Nowadays, it's all different. Most kids don't buy albums anymore; they just tap a button on their cell phones and hear what they want. There's no mystery anymore, either. I remember checking out the rock magazines every month to see who was in the new issue. It was the only way you could see your favorite band if they weren't on a television show. Again, nowadays, kids just have to punch in YouTube on their phones and see anything they want. I think it ruined the mystique.

Any band that sounded and looked good was in my collection. By 1979, I had a huge record collection and wanted to be like my heroes…A ROCK STAR!

Yes, I was hooked. Hook, line and sinker. There was nothing else on this planet that interested me more than music. Even though I couldn't play a single note on the guitar, I played my records loud in my bedroom and pretended I was playing live. I'd sit at the dinner table dripping sweat so much, my mom and Dad thought I was running around outside, but oh, no, no…In my deluded little mind, I just played Madison Square Garden! The only difference was that instead of playing a guitar, I had my rifle from Disney World's Frontierland strapped over my shoulder.

Looking back, since I was sixteen years old, it would have been more beneficial if I had at least started to learn how to play the guitar instead of pretending.

Take A Seat At The Back Of The Train Kid

I was now in high school. It was time to prepare for my future. Unfortunately, my academics suffered as I felt little need for what the schools were teaching. I wasn't bitter; I couldn't blame the high school for not teaching ROCK-N-ROLL 101!

Looking back, I guess I should have been a little more studious, but there was so much going on, and I was concentrating on survival. During my first year in school, I was, of course, just a little 9th-grade greenhorn. I didn't see it that way, but it was hard to convince the 11th and 12th grade bullies.

There were also four types of so-called gangs roaming the halls. The Cowboys, the Surfers, the Blacks, and the Hispanics. I didn't have a problem with any of them. I couldn't care less what color your skin is or where you came from. A good person is a good person, and bad is bad. You shouldn't judge a book by its cover (except for this one, the one in your hands).

Although I had long blonde hair and actually surfed, I had nothing to do with the Surfer gang. One day in the gym locker room, as I closed my locker and tried to haul ass to my next class, I had two black guys try to jump me and give me a hard time. I figured it was because I was a newbie 9th grader, and these guys were going to razz me and show me who's the boss.

Lucky for me, I loved fighting and thrived on bullies. Growing up watching Billy Jack movies and Batman made me think I was invincible, even though I didn't know karate.

Like Batman, I patiently waited for my time to strike. When the opportunity came, I quickly kicked the guy doing all the talking in the groin and pinned the other guy against the wall with my hand, squeezing his throat.

I swear I saw the guy on the floor had tears in his eyes as he held his hands on his smashed private parts, gasping for air. In the midst of threatening the guy I was holding against the wall, the coach and the security guy ran in and stopped it.

From then on, they left me alone. I even became friends with some of their friends. In fact, I had friends in all the gangs except for the Cowboys. The Cowboys thought they were tough with their big 4-wheel drive pickups, cowboy boots, and hats. They even spit dip in Coke cans during class. What a bunch of posers.

The following year, the 10th grade, was looking better for me. I met my girlfriend and future wife, Elaine, and I was talking to some people who had a rock band. All was good until the Cowboys in Elaine's class decided I shouldn't be her boyfriend. One guy even told her they were going to tie me to their truck bumper and drag me down the street.

When she told this to me, I laughed. I wanted her to point the guy out to me while I was walking her to her homeroom class. This went on for days until one day, as we were walking, this guy suddenly popped out from the corner hallway and ran to his classroom, shouting, "I was kidding, I was kidding."

I couldn't keep from laughing as Elaine pointed at him and said he was the cowboy who was going to tie me to the bumper. I didn't bother to pursue the threat. I wasn't a vigilante; I was a Rock-N-Roller.

I found out later that people thought I was some kind of crazy kid who would fight anybody. Seems I had a minor reputation because I was seen a few times stopping delinquent kids between school and McDonald's at lunchtime who were beating up classmates for their lunch money.

I was no bully, but I stood up for the weaker citizens who couldn't stand up for themselves. I've been like that since 1st grade. I owe it all to growing up watching Batman.

With all the high school crap going on, I finally did find a group of long-haired freaky friends who were starting a little band called the Virgin Breakers. Wow! *What a name. I knew right there and then that they would never perform at church carnivals.* I told them I wrote lyrics but couldn't play guitar. They said they wrote songs but not lyrics. I convinced them they needed me, and they fell for it.

For the next few weeks, I went to the guitar player's house so that he could teach me how to play. All this guy did was convince me how bad it is to smoke pot and take drugs. He was more out of it than anything else.

Being raised in a loving family, I knew right from wrong, and although I'm no angel, taking drugs was not for me. My first thought was to get up and leave, but then I reasoned with myself and figured that the rock-n-roll world was full of these types.

I decided to press on. It was comical. He was trying to show me how good he played, but even a rookie like me could tell how badly his guitar was out of tune. The stupid-looking smile on his face while he played reminded me of a newborn baby that had just farted in his diaper.

One day, we somehow got the chance to audition for some school event. I still didn't know how to play, but I stood around with the band and acted like I knew what I was doing while these guys were jamming away, trying to copy their favorite new band called Van Halen.

The guitar player was in la la land, playing his best Eddie Van Halen interpretation while the others bobbed their heads up and down, staring down at their instruments. Besides believing a band needed a good image, I also made a mental note to make sure that if or when I ever learned how to play guitar, I wouldn't keep my head down and stare at my guitar's neck. I thought that was the best way to bore an audience to tears.

Even though I couldn't play a single note, I knew the band didn't feel right. I can't explain how, but when a band clicks, it flows along, and it's a great feeling to be making the sound you're hearing, but when it doesn't click, it feels broken, and no matter how hard you try, it can't be fixed.

When the school administration found out the name of the band, they were canned instantly. The guys thought it was funny, but I took it seriously for some oddball reason. It was probably the frustration of not knowing how to play guitar, and that I knew I was in with the wrong group of guys.

Being a novice, I could hardly call the shots. I knew I was wasting my time with these druggies and moved on. I was glad that I did because the group broke up shortly after I left, not because of me, of course, but because they couldn't make their sound click.

There are so many talented musicians who sound fantastic, jamming away in their bedrooms, plugged into an amp until the neighbors want to kill them. However, being in a band with three or four other musicians is a whole different ball game. Each member has to find that special groove together with the band in order to get that secret ingredient that makes a band click.

I felt good about the experience. I got my foot in the door; all I had to do now was learn how to play guitar and get in with the right bunch of people. I was taking baby steps on the stepping stone to something better.

In the summer of '79, Cheap Trick became one of my favorite groups. I'll tell you more about these guys and how we almost shared the stage with them later in the book.

I also met a guy who didn't let his inability to play guitar get in his way, either. His name was Don. I showed him some lyrics, and we decided to take our extremely limited talent and start a band called Silver Bandits. We practiced harmonizing and were going to be a mix of Jan and Dean and every other act with two lead singers and a sense of humor.

We hung flyers at the grocery store and gas stations that read: *Two singers looking for a band.* I don't know if we were crazy or just plain stupid to put flyers where we did, and of course, nobody called.

We finally decided that we should take lessons and learn how to play guitar. Instead of going to some rockin' instructor whom we could have identified with a bit more, we signed up at a place called The Webster School of Music.

What a mistake! The jack-ass teacher was trying to teach us "Mary Had a Little Lamb" while we wanted to crank up and play "Highway to Hell." The very first thing he wanted me to do was to sit cross-legged so the guitar could sit comfortably in my lap. I told him

I was never in my life able to sit like that without crushing my you-know-whats, and besides, I wanted to wear a guitar down to my knees, not sit down with a guitar in my lap.

Anyway, we took two lessons and convinced ourselves that he didn't know a thing about rock-n-roll, so we quit. We figured we'd just learn to harmonize and become the next sensational singing duo on our own. We'll be a hard-rocking version of Simon and Garfunkel.

While we were working out our mixed-up, muddled-up, shaken-up delusion, Don's niece had a birthday party one Saturday afternoon at his aunt's house, and this was going to be our first big performance. I was oblivious that these little girls were just entering the double-digit age. I just wanted to entertain them and sing into my new microphone.

In my delirious mind, we were playing at the Madison Square Garden. In reality, we were singing Beatles songs in a tiny living room of a small apartment to an eight-track tape, with our voices drowning out the singers on the tape. It was dreadful, but I called it another stepping stone. Thank God there's not a recording of it.

I finally bought a record of a band called the Ramones that got my juices flowing. When they first became popular the year before, I sort of shrugged them off for some reason and thought I'd eventually get around to it and buy their records.

But now I was desperate to be in a rock band. They played simple power chords. Most of their songs didn't have more than three chords. I was convinced that all I needed to know was three chords, and I could start a band like them.

I learned three power chords and practiced until my fingers bled. When I was confident, I showed Don what I had learned and tried to teach him too. We practiced like our lives depended on it, but for some reason, we just couldn't make the chords sound good when we played together.

While Don struggled to get his big fingers in place on the fretboard of his guitar, I finally found two more nutcases to join our calamitous band.

A guy named Alan, w*ho actually knew how to play guitar,* and a friend named Perry on drums. Perry didn't know how to play drums, but he wanted to be a drummer, so he was in. Our first practice together ended with Allen not saying a word. After the first so-called song, he took off his guitar, packed up, and left the building.

A couple of days went by, and we decided to have another practice. I licked my wounds and told Don and Perry we could practice at my house. I'm glad it was there because, as it turned out, I was the only one who showed up. I was fuming until I found out that Don did something stupid again and ended up in jail. I couldn't stop laughing. As for Perry, I don't know what happened, and I never saw him again. He probably ended up in the hospital with ink poisoning because he had a new tattoo drawn with Indian ink every time I saw him.

You had to know Don before you could judge him. He reminded me a lot of Kramer from the Seinfeld show. Not only did he look and act like Kramer, but almost everything he did was against the law. But in his eyes, it seemed ok; he was right, and the world was wrong.

I took it as a sign that nothing would ever get done with trying to get something going with him and moved on. It seemed a little harsh, being that Don was a friend of mine, but I was on a mission to become a rock star, and unfortunately, I couldn't let friendship ruin my dreams. I'm fairly certain this is the reason I haven't spoken to or seen him in more than forty years.

As always, I looked at it as another stepping stone and continued my struggle to get into a rock group. I was still on the right track, able to spot trouble within a band and move on. The Virgin Breakers would never get off the ground with their stupid band name and use of drugs. The Silver Bandits were doomed from the start because…well, we just didn't know how to play.

Ticket To Ride

It would have really come in handy if I had learned the names of the three chords I was playing because one day, I answered an ad in a local rock magazine that read, "Rock band seeks bass player, all original music."

One of the things I dislike about myself is that I often jump at something I want to do without giving much thought to the consequences.

It was the last couple of months of 1981, and I was 18 years old. Time was wasted, and if I was going to be a rock star, it was now or never.

The band was called CHAOS. I went to the audition with my cheap imitation of a Gibson bass guitar and a portable amplifier with a 4-inch speaker. I was either delusional or had balls of steel... I think I had both. Out of the corner of my eye, I could see the bewildered look on the faces as I plugged in my amp. It looked like I was searching for an outlet to plug in my portable radio.

I wasn't even finished plugging the amplifier into the wall when Mike, the guitar player, asked when the last time was that I changed my guitar strings. I looked up at him and seriously replied, "Never, none of them broke." The look on his face was priceless.

He and the rest of the band looked at me as if I were from another planet. There was stunned silence as Mike, the guitar player, proceeded to write down the chords to one of their songs while I tried tuning my ancient strings with their electronic tuner gadget, something I had never seen in my life.

It was comical as I sat there, acting like I knew what I was doing. The strings sounded like a wet bag of mud when I plucked them, *thud-thud, thud-thud, bffft.*

Mike handed me the sheet of paper he had been doodling on, and I had no clue what I was looking at. It was the words to the song, with letters written on top of the words. I had no idea the capital letters were the chords to the song.

I was determined to be in the band, so I played my cards and told them I didn't know chords. I knew sheet music, "A-A-A-B," meant nothing to me.

Damn! Could you believe it! Mike called my bluff and started writing the song down with sheet music! Game over, I lost.

They kicked me out of there faster than a soccer ball. I came to realize something valuable—there are essentially seven foundational chords, each accompanied by their own variations of major and minor forms. This discovery opened up a whole world of musical possibilities for me. All I had to do was learn them. I would learn all the chords and put them over my lyrics, and voila! I will have written a complete masterpiece. I held my head up high and took it as another stepping stone I'd stomped on to reach my goal.

I went home and locked myself in my bedroom for a month or two with a chord chart and learned guitar chords. Like a fog was lifted, it suddenly made sense to me now. I quickly learned what I needed to know and cockily wrote a bunch of songs, incorporating my lyrics with my newly found talent for playing bass guitar.

I heard somebody say a while back that you didn't have to play a million notes to have a good song. If the listener heard it and could walk away humming the tune in his head, it was a good song. I found that to be true.

People could hear a Beatles song for the first time and walk away whistling it. How many Yes or other progressive bands in that genre could have people hear their songs once and walk away with them sticking in their heads? Not many.

Finally, I was ready to rock. Not only that, but I was also cocky enough to place an ad in the local rock magazine to hold auditions and start my own band. The very same day the ad came out, you know who called me!? It's Flash, the lead singer from CHAOS!

He said, "You may not remember me, but I'm the singer from Chaos. You auditioned a few months back."

Not remember! Are you kidding? How could I forget? Their nightmare of auditioning me was my awakening. It was through that perilous audition that I learned chord structure and how to incorporate it into my lyrics. And now he's answering MY ad? Some things are just meant to be, but not before a lot of hard work.

He continued talking and said there was absolutely no way the band would have me back, but if he and I wanted to get together and learn all their songs, they might change their mind. I had nothing to lose except being the lead singer in my own band, but it was worth it.

I could have turned it down and kept working to form my own band or, with a lot of luck, join a rock band in need of a bass player. I chose the latter. Flash and I got together every day for about a month, learning Chaos songs.

I never told him, but Flash taught me a lot about song structure. Not by talking about it, but by the repetitive playing of his songs during this time. This was the thing I desperately needed in order to enhance my songwriting ability. He took the time to teach me what I needed to know to become part of a rock band.

I remember the first time I showed up at Flash's house, he asked if I wanted a beer. I said sure, just to be polite, then he said he was having a Kool-Aid. Great, now I felt like an alcoholic who needed a drink to get the edge off while the leader of the band had a cherry Kool-Aid.

During this month-long experience, we found we had a lot of the same interests. He even liked Alice Cooper more than me!! He built an electric chair in his bedroom that resembled Alice Cooper! It was fantastic. I thought to myself that if I weren't going to be accepted in the band, I would at least become their roadie until my own band got going.

We also liked booze-cruising up and down the beach on Friday nights with the radio blaring our favorite music. He even liked Slade, which blew my mind. I thought I was the only person who liked them on this side of the Atlantic. We became the best of friends in a very short time.

When we got all the songs down tight, it was time to meet the band. Flash called the guys for a rehearsal one Saturday afternoon, assuring them he'd found a capable bass guitar player.

It was showtime. I wasn't a bit nervous because I knew the songs perfectly. I could even pick up from the middle of a song if they wanted.

The band strolled into Flash's parents' living room and set up to play. Looking around, they wondered where the bass player was. Following Flash's instructions, I showed up a half hour later. He figured once they set up, it would be harder to pick up and leave after they saw me trample in like a rookie-bass-playing lunatic.

As I set up, grinning from ear to ear, I ignored the shocked faces and tuned the brand-new strings on my cheap copy of a Gibson SG bass guitar and plugged into my tiny guitar amp.

Mike had a look on his face as if he had just wasted his Saturday afternoon, and Dave, the drummer, gave me the evil eye like he wanted to fight. All this while Flash was in the kitchen stirring a cherry Kool-Aid.

The first song we played was the three-chord song I tried to bluff my way through a few months earlier. All in all, it was about six chords. I stepped back and widened my stance to look like Dee Dee Ramone and prepared for the count-off. The excitement I felt was the same as being on the slow climb of a roller-coaster ride, ready to take the plunge.

As the song began, the electricity flowing through me as I realized I was playing in a band was thrilling! We played the entire set, and it clicked. We were tighter than a small-sized pair of underwear on an elephant.

After the audition, if Mike didn't like it, big deal. I'd punch him in the nose and start my own band. I was on cloud nine and had nothing to lose.

We played non-stop for about half an hour. When we finished, the band had to decide if I was in or out. By the time I was packed up and ready to leave, they welcomed me into the band. YES! 5 years after making my decision to be a rocker, I was in a rock group! Flash, Mike, Dave and me ... look out, world, here we come!

I had this crazy idea that now that I was in a rock group, nothing could go wrong. Ouch! What a mistake. I was young, dumb and fully numb.

We rehearsed every Saturday afternoon in Flash's parents' living room and got the set down tight. During one rehearsal, my tiny guitar amp started making a funny noise, and it sounded like an 18-wheeler gearing down before a stop. How was I supposed to know you couldn't play bass guitar through a tiny guitar amp?

It finally blew up, and I had to go out and buy a real bass amp. I purchased a brand-new Peavey, a 200-watt bass amp that changed my sound 100%. I was as proud as a peacock. Next, I needed a real bass guitar. I know the Fender bass is one of the best, but I thought they looked mind-numbing and weighed a ton. I wanted to look cool as well as have a good guitar, so I kept searching.

I finally found what I was looking for, and it fit my small budget in a music store. It was a black and white Peavey T-40 with a light brown neck and slightly darker fretboard. It looked cooler than cool.

I put it on layaway and stopped in every week with another payment for a couple of months until I paid it off. I would always walk in and make the payment. Then, I would ask the guy to take the bass down from the top shelf and open the case so I could peek at it. He'd roll his eyes and take it down. I would open the case and stare at it, dreaming it was strapped on me and I was rockin' Madison Square Garden.

Now, the band had decent gear, and we were ready to go out and perform. The only problem was, we played our own original songs and there were limited clubs to play in. If you didn't play top 40 hits, you were considered a garage band. Drummer Dave was getting bored and, as always, threatened to quit.

Lucky for us, Flash and Mike heard that a local record store in Miami was going to compile an album of the best Florida indie bands and wanted bands to send their best demo tape for consideration.

On January 2, 1982, we were booked at a well-known studio called BRT Studios to record our demo.

You would think it would be easy for a band ready to take on the world just to show up and do their thing, but the powers of Snafu are overbearing. Dave didn't show up at Flash's parents' house, where we were supposed to meet.

This was before cell phones, so Mike stayed behind in case he showed up and kept calling his house; while Flash and I jumped into the car and sped over to his house; he wasn't there. We went to his favorite bars and still couldn't find him. We went back to his house in case he came home, and he was nowhere to be found.

Finally, walking back to the car and calling him every name in the book, the door of his customized love-machine van swung open, and he stepped out in a daze. We were floored and asked where the hell he'd been, and he just yawned and replied that he fell asleep in his van! We didn't say anything since he was always teetering on quitting the band. We just helped him load up the drums, picked up Mike and made it to the studio like a bat out of hell.

In the studio, Guitar Mike wanted me to use a Fender bass. He said it would be the best sound for the recording. I thought it was a power play and swallowed my pride and played the tree-trunk fender. I didn't complain, and I had to pick my battles. Besides, I was inches away from becoming a rock star. We recorded 5 or 6 songs and went to Burger King to celebrate.

A couple of days after it was mixed, Flash and Mike listened to the tape and decided it sounded too polished for a punk band. I thought it sounded good, but that didn't matter; I was the new guy, and nobody asked for my opinion.

We ended up recording in Flash's parents' living room with a borrowed 4-track tape recorder, and surprisingly, it sounded pretty good.

At the next rehearsal, Flash and Mike changed the name of the band to a single letter of the alphabet...*F*.

I didn't get it. Why would they change the name to *F?* I told them I didn't like it, but it was brushed aside. They knew I wouldn't quit because their songs were the only songs I knew besides my own. Again, I just shut up and continued with my place in the band. I was like a sponge collecting water, soaking up and learning everything I could.

It took a few weeks before I finally got the reasoning for the letter from the group. We were a slice-and-dice, rockin' punk band. The letter F only added to the absurdity.

Next, we needed promo pictures. Dave couldn't be bothered running around all over town posing like punk rockers in alleyways and abandoned buildings, so we got Flash's friend named Pete, to take his place.

He was also a great drummer and played in about three other local bands, so he wore a bag over his head so that he wouldn't be recognized. I thought it was kind of funny because he had a bit of a potbelly, and since he was a popular drummer on the local scene, everybody pretty much knew who he was anyway.

***

One night, when I was cruising to my girlfriend's house, I heard a commercial on the radio promoting the grand opening of a new go-kart track called The Grand Pre-Race-O-Rama.

The relentless promoter in me thought it would be a good idea to contact the owner and convince him that *F* should be the entertainment since I didn't hear anything on the radio about a live band performing at the event.

I called the guy and told him I managed a rock group that was getting ready to release an album. I told him the band had a big following and that they'd be in town that weekend. In those days, there was no YouTube or any social media where he could verify what I said.

He could either tell me to bug off or take his chances on securing a well-known band for his event. He fell for my bluff and booked us right away. Before the weekend, the commercial changed to include the popular rock group *F*. Damn, that was easy…Too easy. I called Flash and told him the great news.

The day before the show, we went down to Miami and picked out some stage clothes. I picked out a tight, leather-looking shirt with a zipper down the middle. It had chrome rings all over it, and it just looked cool. Everybody bought something, but I didn't see what Mike bought until we were heading back up I-95.

He opened his bag and took out a shirt exactly like mine! Sonofabitch! I could have killed him. Flash almost crashed the car because he was laughing so hard.

The night of our first show, I decided I didn't want to look like Mike's twin brother, so I put my new leather shirt on with tight white pants, I looked like David St. Hubbins of Spinal Tap. Guess what!? Mike showed up with white pants, too! We looked like punk rock Everly brothers!

The place was packed to the limit, probably not from people dying to see us, and the go-karts were racing. The local radio station was there promoting the place, and we were ready to set up, only there was no stage.

I spotted the owner, walked over, and introduced myself. He looked thrilled that the place was packed and bought me a beer, probably thinking the band had something to do with the turnout, before telling me he thought it would be a good idea to set up on the grassy island in the middle of the track. What the hell?

After Dave complained about everything, Mike stopped pissing and moaning, and we ran out, dodging go-karts, to set up and play.

What a nightmare, nobody, including us, liked the noise coming out of the speakers. I don't know if it was because of the go-karts speeding past the open microphones or the fact that open-air shows were impossible to make sound good, but it sounded like a cross between a wounded animal and the Texas Chainsaw Massacre with jet airplanes flying over.

Flash, ever the showman, realizes the nightmare and makes the best of the situation. He takes off his leather jacket and starts whacking the go-kart drivers while they whiz by. He looked like a matador in the bull ring.

The audience turned into a booing mob, and I started preparing for a hasty escape. The plan was to finish the last song, pack our stuff, and exit before we got killed. The green-painted streak in Mike's hair didn't help either. He looked like a punk rock princess, waiting for a knight in shining armor to come by and punch him in the head.

We plowed through the crowd easily until some redneck-go-cart-engine-mechanic-looking guy grabbed Mike and tried to rip out the green streak in his hair. I laughed when the guy asked if he was some kind of a fag.

I suppose Mike had the last laugh because three years later, he was in a band called The Gay Cowboys in Bondage. Anyway, to make a long story short, we escaped and vowed never to play in the center of a go-kart track again, a promise easily kept. *Lesson learned: Always work out the details before running out and destroying a good opportunity.*

***

The craziness was too much, and it was …. literally. I was slowly learning that most of the heartache and failure is not limited to outside sources in the music biz trying to destroy your hopes and dreams, but also the internal bullshit that goes on within the band. I acted like I couldn't care less; I was paying my dues and learning everything I could, taking it all in and saving it for later.

Next, Flash and Mike decided we needed stage names. Flash already has his stage name (real name Angelo). Mike became Ravenous Gangrene, and I was Bruce Beast. Dave the drummer remained Dave the drummer because he wanted to continue being miserable and boring.

I was the new guy who barely knew how to play my instrument, so I had very limited say in the band. But if I were calling the shots, I would never have a drummer like Dave in my band because it brought morale down. To me, it doesn't matter if you get along with the guys in the band or not, but everybody must at least have the same goal.

Elaine and me in the beginning of the rockin' train ride

Virgin Breakers faded out. Now I'm back on the horse.

Recording with F

Good Times, Bad Times

It was the spring of 1982, and I was 19 years old. I kept thinking my big break better happen soon before I got too old. I was quickly learning the ups and downs of being a struggling rock–n–roller. We performed in all the places that supported the original music scene and dealt with all the thoughtless demands, including over-bookings and crappy time slots.

We also continued having problems with Dave not showing up for rehearsals and generally just being a pain in the ass.

We played a headlining show in Miami on April 13th, and it finally clicked. The audience loved the punk rock-infused slice-and-dice noise of F. Finally, and the wheels were rolling.

Dave was still the rusty wheel that kept the train from running smooth, but we steamed ahead slowly. We had bookings, and he was making all kinds of outrageous and stupid demands before he finally quit the band just before we had an important gig lined up in Miami. A popular South Florida radio station was on hand at the event, and now we had no drummer.

A week before the show, Flash and I went to Dave's house and promised he'd be well paid, and we'd meet his outrageous demands. I think the funniest thing was when he finally said he'd do it if there were a 5-minute break between songs. I can't imagine a punk band, or any band for that matter, standing on stage between songs for less than 10 seconds. Flash wanted to kill him, but I quickly cut in and assured him that it'd be no problem to stand there for five minutes between songs while he relaxed and sipped his drink.

The night of the big show, Dave was all happy and thinking he was going to breeze through the setlist, relax for five minutes between songs and leave with a pocket full of cash. If he carried a gun, I don't think I'd be sitting here writing this book.

Flash shaved his head in a Mohawk style; Mike sprayed a little green stripe in his hair again, and I wore a black t-shirt with the sleeves ripped off and black jeans. There was no way I was going to look like the twin of the green stripe-haired Ravenous Gangrene.

We played louder, harder and faster than ever before, with about two seconds between songs. The audience loved it, and it was one of the best shows we ever played.

During the show, I'd strut over to Dave and couldn't stop grinning, and the poor bastard looked like he was going to explode. Every time we locked eyes, he was shouting something, and I would just smile and point at my ear to let him know I couldn't hear a word he was saying. The poor guy looked like he was going to have a stroke. There was nothing he could do. He was trapped behind those drums and had no choice but to keep playing or stop and look like a fool.

After the show, Dave didn't say a word. He packed up his drums and headed out the back door, never to be seen again.

***

We got lucky and didn't skip a beat. Flash and Mike decided it was time to get our own rehearsal space. I'm sure it was because Flash's parents were going deaf from our practices in their living room. We rented a warehouse in the worst section of town and started auditioning drummers.

A nutcase named Tom became our new drummer. He was a white guy with an afro, and he reminded me a little of Bob Ross, the 'happy painter' guy on television.

I don't remember being asked to join in on the auditioning process, and I wasn't a bit surprised. It was very apparent that good 'ol Mikey thought of me as the underling. Of course, I couldn't blame him for what I put him through when I auditioned.

But suddenly, we had a new drummer sitting behind his 5-piece, yellow drum kit. To me, with that cool-looking afro, he looked like he should have been the drummer for Sly and the Family Stone or Grand Funk Railroad, not a punk rock band called F. I started to wonder why Flash didn't seem too concerned about our new drummer's image.

Mike and I dressed the part of punk rockers while Flash took it to the next level and destroyed everything around him when we played live. The truth of the matter didn't dawn on me until a few months later when I realized that Flash couldn't care less about what the guys in the band looked like; they were the backup band, and he was F.

The funny thing about Tom was, for one reason or another, he just loved to hear Mike scream out in pain. He'd always catch him off guard and give his nipple a twist until he screamed. Flash and I tried to hold back our laughter out of respect for Mike's pain, but every time it happened, we'd end up cracking up, which only made him even madder.

***

It was now May 1982. Flash and Mike came to rehearsal and announced that F was one of the bands selected to be on the compilation album. I was floored. In just a few short months, I went from learning how to play guitar in my bedroom to being in a rock band featured on a vinyl album!

The album was called *Florida, The Land That Time Forgot*. The song we had on the album was "I saw your vision in a three-car collision," the same song I tried to bluff my way through a few months earlier.

When we secured the song on the album, my guess is that was the reason we got better bookings with better bands in the lineup.

The newest original music club to be seen and heard in was called Finders Lounge. It was located under a hotel on the beach between Hollywood and Miami. Punk rock giants Black Flag and The Misfits graced the stage, and we played there steadily for the next 3 months.

One night, a local guy who managed one of the best bands in Florida, with an album out and songs on the radio, came to talk to Flash. Probably wanted to manage us, but we'll never know. Every time he walked over to talk, Flash turned and ran away. I don't know why, but probably just to piss him off, or maybe it was a punk rock thing.

During this time, I had attached a large shark tooth between the head and neck of my bass guitar. If any of the punk rock stage destroyers tried to smash my amp, they would feel the pain as the shark tooth sank into their body.

On one of these crazy nights, Flash and I smashed into each other on stage, and the tooth bit him on the side of his face. As the blood dripped down his face, the crowd went crazy. They cheered and threw their fists in the air as the devil himself had just made a grand entrance. They had no idea it was real blood.

By this time, Flash had a reputation for smashing things onstage. F was getting more and more popular, and people began to show up at our rehearsals. The rehearsals became Friday night events, and the punkers were very encouraging in the destruction department.

The warehouse was in the worst part of town, which even the police tried to avoid, which only made us crank up the music louder, believing they would not show up.

We put egg crates on the walls to absorb the sound, but it was useless. We still sounded like a riot from a mile away. We'd have the warehouse door open, burning through the set list while Flash smashed rows of televisions and mirrors.

Friday nights became punk rock headquarters at the warehouse until the cops would eventually come over and shut us down for the evening.

It was around this time that I tried to get some of my songs on the setlist. With Tom in the band, I was no longer the new guy, and I felt it was time for my songs to see the light of day. It was easier said than done because Flash and Mike were a team. Flash wrote the lyrics and the song structure, and Mike tweaked it on guitar. There was no place for another songwriter in the band, and they didn't want to hear any of my stuff.

After my persistent attempts to include my songs, Flash added my song called *"Death To All"* from my escalating catalog. He probably did it to shut me up, but I didn't care until we sped it up so fast that it ended up being the shortest song in the set list (38 seconds). Whatever, I figured it was a start, and it did get a good reaction at the shows. It felt good to hear my song, and it kept me happy for a while.

I Rode The Rock Train

On August 16, 1982, the compilation album was released. Amazing! Me, Bruce Norris (I mean Beast) was on a record album! I'm a recording artist! It was one of the proudest moments in my life. It was sold in record stores everywhere. I remember walking into a store with my friends and family, making sure they saw it on display. The record sold fairly well *(in my mind),* and we made two cents for every album sold. So what? I'm a recording star! I never saw the money anyway; I wonder how much we made.

When the record came out, we started getting more bookings. People knew the band now, and the audience was starting to grow a little bigger. I knew we were going to hit the big time sooner or later, and I was savoring the feeling of having my picture on a record album. And it was the greatest feeling in the world.

We were now opening shows for national punk bands like the Misfits. I thought *we were on our way, and it was only a matter of time before we'd become rock stars!*

We were added to open the show for the Misfits about two hours before showtime. Again, I wasn't told, but I figured the original opening act was canceled at the last minute. With all the hustle to get our equipment up and running on the stage, my bag of guitar chords and picks went missing, and Mike, the professional, didn't have an extra chord for me to use.

With a half-hour before showtime, Flash and I went upstairs and knocked on the Misfits' hotel room door. A security guard opened the door and looked at us like we were groupies or something and said, "Only one of you in here at a time."

"What the hell? No," I said. "I'm the bass player opening for you guys, and somebody snatched my guitar chord," and I asked if they might have a spare. He let us into the room, and we saw the band quickly change into their punk rock demeanor and look bored as they sat on the bed, pretending to read comic books.

They looked cool. All dressed in black with their hair in a ponytail in front of their faces. Black makeup under their eyes. I liked it, as I said earlier, I liked bands that dressed for showbiz. I waited for the guitar player to finish reading his comic book and asked if he could lend me a guitar chord. He responded like a true punk rocker and said, "Hell yeah."

After the show, we watched the Misfits talking to their fans as their followers gifted them with comic books. Hell, I didn't know that was part of their schtick. I would have given them an interesting Batman comic to show my appreciation.

I thought *things were looking good, and with hard work, we'd be on our way.* Then it happened, and internal problems sprang up again. Tom never cared for the destruction we made at the warehouse and the shows. He told Flash to stop smashing things and slow down the songs. Flash didn't bother arguing—he just nodded along as he agreed, then went on to destroy everything in sight at the very next show.

Tom didn't see the big picture; it was part of the show, and the fans expected it. Finally, after the destruction of more televisions at the warehouse extravaganzas, Tom quit. He packed his drums, tweaked Mike's nipple until he screamed out in pain for the last time and was gone.

Great, now we need another drummer. Drummers were hard to find, and it looked like there were none to be auditioned.

To keep things moving, Mike decided to switch to drums. There was a snotty-nosed-punk guitar player named Ken who had been hanging around the warehouse for a while. Suddenly, he was the new guitar player. This was the beginning of the end for me in the band. Again, I had no say in it, and this time, it pissed me off.

Our sound turned into what sounded like a buzzsaw. It was hard to tell one song from the other. I had lost all interest in staying in the band, but I wasn't ready to jump ship yet. I was biding my time. I thought *it was just a matter of time until Flash agreed with me that we sounded horrible.*

As I expected, Ken influenced Mike to play twice the speed of sound, and it sounded like garbage. With Mike pounding on the drums like a jackhammer, the set that we rehearsed to get nice and tight was now just a loose, chainsaw-sounding mess. I never complained before because I was honing my skills, but now I was in a band that I didn't want any part of. I was disappointed that my friend Flash had turned in this direction.

Out of the blue, we got an offer from somebody I knew to play at a backyard party. We had to learn 2 sets of classic rock songs, and I *thought it would be a good way to tighten up the band. I also thought that if Flash wanted to play this gig, maybe, just maybe, the band would get away from the speed-punk crap.* We rehearsed the classics, and things seemed to look brighter. Even Ken sounded good on guitar.

I was finally feeling good about being in the band again when I was blindsided. We got to the party early to set up and noticed a bunch of elderly people filling the backyard. One lady was probably in her eighties and sat next to one of the giant speaker cabinets.

It was 8 o'clock, and we were ready to rock. We started the set with *"Some*body to Love" by Jefferson Airplane. The poor lady next to the speaker almost died on the spot. I think that the first chords of the song blew her ears out as she stood up and screamed, holding her hands to her ears. It was kind of funny, and we couldn't keep from laughing until a gang of the elderlies rushed the stage and tried to shut us down.

It didn't take long to realize that we weren't going to last long at the party, so we started playing the songs to fit our style, punk rock versions complete with buzz saw sound. Finally, the elders found the main power, shut us down and threw us out on the street. We left the scene after they paid us and decided that backyard parties were not for F.

As the months wore on, the bookings became far few as original rock clubs began disappearing. The warehouse rehearsals became our main live shows, and everybody but me was having a blast.

By now, I had a backlog of songs that looked like they'd never see the light of day, and I was itching to sing them in my own band. I had to do something if I was going to make it to the big time, and it didn't look like F was going to get me there.

By the end of '82, it was time for me to move on. I was proud of what I accomplished in one year and would miss our legendary Friday night booze cruises when we swore we'd stick together through thick and thin. But now I had to get out. I saw it as yet another stepping stone on my way to becoming a rockstar.

I walked away, wondering what we should have done better. When we finally got it together and found our audience, we probably should have tried to talk to The Misfits manager, or even the manager we ran from, to see what we could do and if they could help get us on tour somewhere. Punk rock was prime, and we should have jumped on it.

Slow Ride

1983 was a tough year for my rock-n-roll dreams. After leaving F, I *thought it would be easy to get my own band together.* I met and rehearsed with tons of guitarists, and I started to realize the problem might've been my own limitations on bass. I was playing Ramones style while the guitar players sounded like Led Zepplin. I practiced and learned more chords in my bedroom, but things just weren't clicking.

One day, I was talking to my friend Jim, yes, the same guy who introduced me to the Bay City Rollers 8 years earlier. Out of the blue, he said he wanted to learn to play drums. Great, let's do this! I thought *I could give him a crash course in drumming like F gave me on bass guitar.* He purchased a brand-new set of drums, and we planned to practice at F's warehouse until he got the basics down.

I asked Flash if it would be possible, and he told me I'd have to see Mike because he held the lease. When I was playing in F, I always felt like a flunky musician around Mike. Probably because I tried to join his band when I didn't know how to play guitar, but that was then, and this was now.

Mike approved but didn't give me a spare key. That would be too convenient. Instead, I had to go to his house to pick up the key to rehearse at the warehouse. This turned out to be a two-hour workout before we played a single note. I had to stop by and pick up Jim, load his drums, my bass amp and guitar into my cool-looking, bright yellow Baja bug, squeeze into the driver's seat and drive about 10 miles to Mike's house, pick up the warehouse key, drive across town to the warehouse, unload, set up, practice, tear down, load up, drive back to Mike's and drop off the key, take Jim home, unload his drums, drive home and unload my gear. It would have been so much easier if I had a key made, but it was another one of Mike's silly games. I quit F, and he made it known that he was in control. I didn't complain. I was paying my dues. It was just another step on my way to rock n roll greatness. This, too, shall pass once I become a rock star.

The problem that didn't even cross my mind was that Jim never got better with the drums. It started sounding worse as time went on. I didn't stop to think that a key ingredient was that you had to want it bad enough to get better. I think that once he found out how much work it was, he just lost interest.

Finally, I had to tell my best friend of 8 years that we had to stop. It didn't sound good and never would. It was hard to tell him, and I think it left a little dent in our friendship, but it was never going to click. I had to make an unscheduled stop at the next train station so Jim could exit.

I looked at it as another stepping stone on the path of rock n roll. Since I was 20 years old, another thought crept into my delusional mind. What if I don't become a rock star? Holy crap! That thought never crossed my mind either, but now it did.

In 1984, I decided to enroll in a technical school and learn about air conditioning so I'd have something to fall back on just in case the rock-n-roll train didn't make it through the tunnel.

One day, I'm sitting in class reading the textbook, and the word "remedy" appears in a sentence. It hit me like a bolt of lightning. What a great name for a rock band.

As I was dreaming my life away and going to a trade school in case my dream didn't come true, I married my beautiful girlfriend of

4 years. After dating for so long, Elaine told me in so many words, "It's now or never, big boy." I was trying to delay until I was a rock star, and thank God I didn't wait. I would be lost without her. Rock-n-Roll kept my soul alive; Elaine kept my heart pounding. I needed both to survive.

As I was cruising through the class, learning about air conditioners and hoping I'd become a rock star sooner rather than later, I became friends with a classmate named Mike. You'd think I would have learned my lesson, but out of the blue, he tells me he always wanted to learn how to play bass guitar and be in a rock group.

Before I could think of what I said, I told him I could teach him how to play and that I would switch to guitar. When he agreed, we started rehearsing at the apartment where my new wife and I lived. I could write a book about Elaine and me, but I think the greatest love story ever told has already been written.

Things were going well with the rehearsals, and Mike learned the chords like a seasoned pro. Now, it was time to add a drummer. Auditioning drummers was a nightmare. Good drummers thought they were too good to be in the band, and bad drummers were just…bad.

I decided to bring my little brother Eric to rehearse with us until we found a drummer. Eric was always drumming on the table, chairs and everything else he could find, so I *thought he could keep rhythm for the time being.* Since he was only 15, we knew we'd have to replace him because he was too young to get into the clubs.

I was still able to get the warehouse key from Guitar Mike so we could rehearse at F's warehouse, only this time, we had limited use of the drums. Eric was allowed to play the bass, snare and the floor tom.

From there, we had to improvise. We used metal trash can lids for symbols, and, believe it or not, they sounded better than the last time I played in F.

We rehearsed three times a week for a couple of months, and our 3-piece band started sounding like a tight little unit. Eric really got into the drums, and he suddenly sounded better than the last two drummers who played in F when I was still a member.

Mike's bass playing became tight with the drums and together, they accidentally fell into their own unique groove. He was also great at learning new songs. Once he learned a song, he knew it forever. He was like a machine. With Eric and Mike holding down the rhythm, I was the only pitfall in the band with my sloppy guitar playing while singing at the same time. But that was ok. With hard work, I would get better.

One day, Eric did something to solidify his membership in the band. He purchased his own set of drums. There was no way Mike and I could tell him to leave if we found a drummer. He became THE drummer. Even though he was too young to get into clubs, we figured we'd cross that bridge when we got there. That was it, Mike, Eric and I were The Remedy.

***

By November 1984, we bade farewell to F's warehouse and moved our rehearsals to a place called T.A.M. studio. The place belonged to an all-female band and their manager. I met and became friends with them while in F.

I'm not going to mention their name because, as I sit and write this book, I went out to see the band leader out playing with her latest band, and she forgot who I was! After all we'd been through with our bands, she forgot who I was! The funny thing is, she remembered Elaine. Surprised and disappointed, I blame the booze and drugs, not her peanut brain.

Now that I didn't have to beg Mike for the key anymore, The Remedy could just show up and focus on rehearsing without the hassle.

On January 19, 1985, we were ready to rock. We rehearsed our setlist so many times that I think we could have played it backwards. We were ready to set the world on fire, but quickly found out there weren't too many clubs to play original music in at the time.

We rented a place called Roarke Hall in the city of Sunrise and had F and another local band added to the bill with us. A week before the show, we posted flyers all over town and in record stores. Our first show was a success, and Eric didn't have to sneak into a club.

Since the show was a success and even got a write-up in a rock magazine called Gold Coast Live, we were able to be added to the rotation of original bands playing at a place called Flynn's on Miami Beach. We were rockin' with the popular bands on a regular basis.

The first time at Flynn's was a make-or-break situation. Eric was only 16 years old and couldn't play in clubs. No problem, we were on the bill with our friends, the all-girl band, and they let us borrow their makeup. We added a mustache and whiskers to Eric's face. He kept a low profile, blending in with the dark atmosphere, and we managed to pull it off. Eureka!

We continued playing there in steady rotation. The stage was about four feet off the ground, and one night, when Mike was finished setting up, he jumped off the stage to grab a beer and broke his ankle.

Like a trooper, he drank until the pain went away and hopped along when we played our set.

Playing at Flynn's was also the first time I used a wireless to plug into my guitar. We were on the bill with the all-girl band, and one of the members wanted me to try it out. I felt like a dog without a leash. During one of my extremely limited guitar solos, I shambled off the stage and did the Chuck Berry shuffle on top of the connecting bar. It was the coolest feeling dancing around people's drinks. While I was doing that, the lights in the entire club switched to black light, and I was happy to see all those bright, glow-in-the-dark, smiling teeth looking up at me. When I finally reached the end of the bar, I fell to my knees in front of a bunch of ladies and split my pants at the crotch. The black light made my underwear look like a beacon of rock-n-roll! We nearly died laughing.

All in all, we had good shows at Flynn's and kept getting return bookings. Two months after the successful show we put together at Roarke Hall, we decided to rent it again and put on a bigger show. This time, since we wanted to pack the place full, we added 3 popular bands, including F, that we knew could draw a crowd to open for us. Once they were finished, I crossed my fingers and hoped the crowd would stay for us.

Remember the old saying, "Be careful what you wish for?" Well, it sure rang true that night.

One thing I didn't take into account was the downtime. Waiting for your turn to hit the stage. We had 3 bands ahead of us that played a 45-minute set each. Fifteen minutes later, the next band played. We had 3 hours to sit and wait. As we waited, we drank tons of beer and were happy to see the place was packed full.

I Rode The Rock Train

When it was almost time for us to go on, Mike was nowhere to be found. I finally slipped out the back door and walked to the front of the hall and found him smashing the hood of his truck in a violent rage and screaming out that somebody stole his special cooler of beer. I've never seen somebody go crazy like that when their beer was stolen. I burst out laughing. When I noticed he wasn't kidding, I had to jump on his back and hold his arms down to keep him from beating up his truck. Then it struck me: good 'ol Mike had to have taken some drugs that were offered so leisurely backstage. At that point, I pushed him away from his dented truck and lectured him in my drunken state.

When he finally settled down and said he'd be ok to play the show, I gave him a puzzled look and thought, *damn right, you're going to play because if you don't, I will beat you worse than you beat your truck.*

When we went on, it was great. The place was still packed to the limit, and our set was surprisingly tighter than tight. Halfway through the set, I couldn't help but notice there was a mosh pit, and the audience started looking like a rugby match. We had a song called "Bad Boys Are Back," and I half-heartedly told the moshers to take the rumble outside where they could really tear each other up.

During the next song, we saw people leaving and couldn't understand why they suddenly didn't like us. Our last song was cut short when a guy from another band rushed over and said there's trouble, and we better get the hell out of there.

We wasted no time packing up. Flash and his guitar player, Keith, helped us load up and make our escape. When we drove past the front of the hall, we saw police, fire rescue and paramedics out front with their lights flashing. When I asked what happened, Flash said that I told the crowd to have a rumble outside, and sure enough, they did. I was relieved to know they didn't walk out because my band stunk, but just as quickly, I was horrified to think I started a riot. Then again, I can't believe they listened to me. All I can say is...Rock N' Roll!

***

Our motto was simple. We would play anytime, anyplace, anywhere.

It seemed like a good motto for a hungry band, but it wound up biting us on the butt a few times. One such time was when we were invited to play at a high school party at some rich kid's house.

Remembering the backyard fiasco when I was in F made me think twice. I told them it would probably be too loud and the cops would be there in minutes. I couldn't change their minds, and we wound up doing it.

Well, I was right. We showed up and set up by the pool area and proceeded to blow away some eardrums. Halfway through the first set, the police showed up and threatened to arrest us if we continued to play a single note. I forgot to mention that we drank a lot of beer, which probably gave Mike the idea to pound out one last "single" note on his bass guitar.

The kids erupted in laughter as I watched Mike get attacked by an officer. Believe it or not, the other officers were also laughing. Before things got out of control, the police just unplugged our amps and threatened to take us to jail if we continued playing.

I can't remember if we got paid or not, but if we didn't, we drank enough beer to cover our fee and then some. The way I saw it was that it was another stepping stone on our way to becoming rock stars.

***

After I left F, they played around for a few months with the buzzsaw sound before Flash got fed up and replaced everybody.

I remember one Friday night when we were out booze-cruising, Flash suddenly said we had to drive to Miami because F was recording in some studio that night. I thought *to myself about the time when drummer Dave did that when I was in F.* I took it that Flash completely lost interest in the guys in the band because we never ended up at the studio, and Flash looked like he couldn't care less.

Rumor had it that he quit the band, but since he was F, I'm pretty sure he replaced everybody. I think the band continued playing as The F Boys until Mike, with the green stripe in his hair, formed The Gay Cowboys in Bondage. Don't ask, I won't tell.

F's new guitar player was a guy named Keith, and it was his garage that they fixed up to rehearse and record in.

Since The Remedy had been playing out now for a few months, we thought it was time to record a ten-song cassette. Since we'd been playing out with the songs we wanted to record, we knew the songs perfectly and didn't waste time while recording them. In fact, we did the entire recording in eleven hours.

During the process, I asked Keith if he'd like to record guitar solos for some of the songs. He said he'd love to, and by next week, he should have some good ideas ready to record. To his surprise, I told him that he had to lay down the solos now and make it spontaneous because that's what rock-n-roll is all about.

He gave me a look that said exactly how dumb I was being, then laid down the solos right there on the spot. And just like that, The Remedy's first recordings were done in 11 hours—basic tracks, vocals, backing vocals, solos, and mixing—all wrapped up in a single day.

***

It was time to add another guitar player. I was pretty good at playing rhythm guitar, but just couldn't be bothered to learn all about playing solos. We auditioned some Jimmy Page wannabees and wound up with a lead guitarist named Kevin.

Kevin had a moustache and reminded me of a hippie freelancer who parachuted down from the Jefferson Airplane and was transported 20 years into the future. Our band image was a decidedly simple but effective one. We looked and sounded dangerous. It certainly wasn't an original look, but it worked; we wore black pants and black sleeveless shirts. In my mind, that's what rock-n-roll should look like. Don't forget, this was 1985. Remember what the rock stars on MTV wore? Well, we were going to bring back their heroes.

Kevin, on the other hand, wore loose-fitting bell-bottom black pants and whatever color button-down shirt with long sleeves he wanted. To top it off, he wore a headband to keep the sweat out of his eyes.

We should have taken him aside and explained the image we wanted to project. Well, I thought, *maybe if he sticks around long enough, he will notice that he looked out of place and wanted to get with the program, but he never did.*

I think I was lucky when Eric and Mike came into the fold. Like me, when I started, they had no clue what to expect until we put in the hard work and came up with our own unique sound. There's something good to be said about new musicians if you put in the extra work. They don't start with attitudes. They must earn them. For the short term, they just want to learn the songs and see what's next.

We were definitely on the right track. Two things I would have changed, though. Since we had an image and walked in and out of clubs like a gang, we should have insisted that the new guitar player dress the same. As I still believe, image is key.

The other thing that most likely hampered our good judgment was the alcohol. I don't know how it started, but we drank more beer than Oktoberfest in Germany.

The Remedy, Rockin' 4th of July show '86

1st show with The Remedy

The Remedy wins trophy in Battle of the Bands

Train Kept A Rollin' All Night Long

It was the city of Sunrise's 4th of July Celebration weekend, and we were on the bill to participate in the weekend-long battle of the bands contest. I always thought Battle of the Bands shows were a cheap way of getting free live entertainment, but we played anyway. We didn't care if we won or lost. We were there for the exposure. Where else could an original rock band play at an outdoor event in front of hundreds of people?

We played the Friday night and won the preliminaries, which allowed us to move forward to the main competition on Saturday night. Great! We get to play in front of the masses again, I thought. We were paying our dues, and it was another stepping stone on the long and winding road to Rocksville.

When we arrived on Saturday, we were met by city officials who told us flat out that because of the riot, we started 4 months earlier at Roarke Hall, there was no way we were going to win the first-place trophy. I guess they wanted to see our faces all broken up and feeling miserable, but we just raised our eyebrows and tried not to laugh. As I said, we couldn't care less, and we just wanted to play for our ever-growing audience.

At the end of the night, they wound up giving us a 3rd place trophy. I guess they showed us. We still couldn't care less; we cherished the fact that we had another chance to perform for hundreds of people again on a Saturday night.

Eight months after Mike, Eric and I dreamed about putting the band together, our 10-song album was released on cassette to the local record stores and the local original rock magazine called Gold Coast Live for review.

We were thrilled. Eric and Mike were a little angry when they walked into the main music store for local bands and saw a red sticker on our cover reading, The Remedy, featuring an ex-bass player from F. I didn't care, and the store had to do what it had to do to sell music. Everybody knew F, but The Remedy? Not so much.

***

Since our path was led by our new motto, "Anytime, Anyplace, Anywhere," we ended up playing a talent contest at a bar called the Rendezvous. We also thought talent contests were a step lower than the Battle of the Bands, another ploy for free entertainment. But we were a new band and wanted people to see us. The club was packed, and we were going to blow their ears off. We were paying our dues.

There we were, sitting at the bar guzzling beer before showtime, when the club introduced the next act...a stripper. As we turned to watch the fleshy surprise for inspiration, I was floored to see the naked lady was none other than my neighbor! She lived in the apartment downstairs from ours! Elaine was sitting next to me when she came off stage and sat next to me on the other side. We tried to look nonchalant as we congratulated her for putting on such a fine show. I didn't want to cause a scene, so I kindly asked her to get her left nipple off my elbow.

All in all, it was another crazy night and another stepping stone. We also won second place. I was too drunk to know who won first, probably the nipple queen.

With no clubs to play in, we kept playing in the Battle of the Bands shows. I saw them as an easy promotion. We'd play a half-hour set of original music and spread the name around. It was a no-brainer. We didn't have to promote our show and put up flyers because the audience was guaranteed to be there. Our only job was to show up and blow their eardrums out.

It was a no-brainer; our next show was another Battle of the Bands, this time, inside a mall. Great, lots of people.

We showed up looking like a gang, most of us anyway. Dressed in our black pants and black, sleeveless shirts and black sneakers, and with our stripped-down, hard-rockin' songs, we could do no wrong. We came to conquer. Three out of the four of us did.

Kevin showed up with bell-bottom black pants, a white button-down shirt and a 4-inch headband wrapped around his head. Holy crap! He looked like a lost hippie from Woodstock!

We gave him the riot act and proceeded to deafen every ear in the mall. After the show, some of the guys in the other bands asked why we were the loudest. I just shrugged my shoulders and didn't have the heart to tell them that we tipped the soundman a few bucks to make us sound as loud as *The Who*.

***

The first 8 months of the new band were beyond my dreams. I was now singing lead and playing rhythm guitar in a band we formed from scratch. We had a growing fan base and had a 10-song cassette out, and had an interview with the local rock magazine. Everything was looking good, and we were ready for the next step. Then came our first hiccup.

It was Labor Day weekend, and we were booked to play in a club called Mothers. I should have known by the name of the club, but we didn't realize it was a lesbian club until we got there. Of course, we would have played there anyway, but my band photographer-wife would probably have stayed clear.

Elaine was fighting off the ladies left and right until our friends from the all-girl group that I mentioned earlier, who was also on the bill, snatched her up and told the muffin monsters she was with them. I couldn't stop laughing.

But the thing that made us want to kill Kevin, well, there were a couple of things that night, but there was a song he wrote that was completely embarrassing to play.

I didn't plan it this way, but I wrote and sang all the songs. I always encouraged other members of the band to write and sing so we could all be equal, but it just didn't work out that way. I was glad when Kevin had a song, but it sure as hell didn't fit the band. His song was called "The Grey Knight." That's right, knight, like in the King Arthur days, to make matters worse, I had to sing it.

Here we were playing blistering, stripped-down rock songs about good times and sex, and then we cut to a slow song about a Knight crying. I never even knew what he was crying about. It wasn't very comfortable. As I sang the song, I saw the raised eyebrows in the audience and made it clear that this was a new song by Kevin. It was like a comedy act to break the blistering tempo of our set. By this point, he was already somewhat separate from the rest of the band, and we just didn't have the guts to fire him.

Another nail in his coffin that night was when he loudly tuned his strings between songs, B-ding, B-ding, B-ding. Ugh, it drove us crazy, and he knew it. We were used to letting the last chord of the songs ring out while Eric counted off the next song. A couple of weeks later, we finally kicked him out of the band.

***

With still not too many places for original music bands to play, our next show was a talent contest at a swanky place on the Intracoastal Waterway called the Riverwatch Lounge in Fort Lauderdale. A radio station sponsored it called 98 Gold, and their wacky DJ was the MC.

Again, we couldn't care less if we won or not. To us, it was another chance to showcase the band and get out in front of more people.

What a mess the show turned out to be. Since we had to haul our equipment through a long parking lot and upstairs, we wore shorts and regular shirts to set up so that when it was time to go on stage, our black rockin' clothes wouldn't be sweat-soaked. After setting up, the soundman wanted a sound check. As we did the sound check, the nutcase DJ from the radio station heard our instruments, and he turned on his microphone and announced, "Ladies and Gentlemen…please welcome The Remedy!

For a split second, we looked like deer in the headlights. I was thrilled to see Eric and Mike acknowledge the crowd and were ready to rock. Seconds later, even though we were dressed like roadies, we were pumping out our ear-splitting originals, to the dismay of the elder boat people and yuppy tourists. Most of the yachties ran for cover while the few others rocked out. I treated it as paying my dues while riding the Rock Train to Rocksville.

***

Eleven months of playing with our motto, "Anytime, Anyplace, Anywhere," we managed to get a good following and figured now was the time to stop playing ill-advised places and concentrate on expanding our horizons, especially after the mess at our last show.

The first thing we did was get another lead guitar player. Tom was his name, and trouble was his game. He was recommended by our friends from the all-female band.

Tom was a great guitar player with a nasty drug habit. I figured that if he could play and not do his drugs around me, we'd be all right. I quickly found out that he was a complete, unreliable space cadet from a planet called Yeranus.

You would think the red flag would go up when he failed at the very first thing on our itinerary, but in his case, the red flag was always up at full mast.

We were booked to go to a studio where a company called United Video Productions wanted to film The Remedy along with 15 other rock bands for a T.V. show on South Florida talent. We were thrilled to test out our new guitar player, and Tom made our songs sound ten times better; the only problem was that he didn't show up.

Of course, by now, we were used to lead guitar players coming and going, so we were well prepared to play as a three-piece band.

When we played at the studio, they filmed 3 songs, and we played them perfectly. Wow, I thought, *three years of struggling to make it and now we're being filmed for a T.V. show! The Rock Train was picking up speed*, and I thought *I'd be a rock star soon, better be because I was 22 years old.*

As it turned out, I never heard anything more about the television show or the company that filmed us. Nothing ever came of it. As for Tom, we found out that he was terrified of playing onstage and chickened out on his way to the studio!

***

In December of '85, we started recording our second album at Triangle Studio, which our friends, the all-girl band, owned. It was also where we rehearsed, formerly known as T.A.M. studio.

This is where Tom's weirdness really kicked in. When he finally arrived, he mumbled incoherently and looked pale as a ghost. I don't know what kind of drugs he took, but he couldn't even play at the sessions. He wanted to be the producer. What the hell? We'd give it a try. Surprisingly, he did a great job, and the songs sounded fantastic.

This time, we didn't rush the recording in 11 hours. It took more than 11 weeks. After Eric, Mike and I recorded the basic tracks to all 10 new songs, Tom would let us hear it a few times to make sure we liked it, then disappear with the tape for a few days.

I would call and ask when he thought he might put the solos on, and he would just shrug it off and say he's working on it. I'm the kind of guy who wants things done now. "Do it now. Tomorrow's too late" is my thinking. But I had to bite my tongue because I was thinking of the big picture, and what he had done so far sounded great.

January came and went, and Tom was still the hermit working on the tape. We had not played a show in 2 months, and we were feeling like rats trapped in a cage.

Finally, in February, Tom comes strolling in with the completed tape. He wanted to do his solos on his own, so we couldn't give him feedback. I could just picture him lying on the floor, drugged out of his mind and recording solos and fill-ins. But I had to give credit where credit was due. Tom's solos and guitar playing were phenomenal.

I still encouraged others in the band to write and sing their own songs. I wanted the band to be one for all and all for one, everybody being equal.

Tom wrote a killer song. After Kevin gave us the Grey Knight in shining armor song, Tom had a song called "Daddy's Little Girl." What the hell? What a pervert! And, of course, I had to sing it. The words to the chorus are, "She's too young, too young to know. Daddy's little girl couldn't tell him no." Complete with harmonies, no less. How creepy can it get? We kept the song on the new album because the music was awesome, probably the best on the record.

I had to swallow my thoughts and move on. If it was going to be one for all and all for one, I had to let the drugged-up, perverted, reptilian guitar extraordinaire have his song.

Now, all we had to do was mix the tape. He wanted to do it by himself, and that's where we drew the line. Not a chance, pumpkin. We all need to be there for the mix.

Each time we tried to get together and mix the tape, Tom didn't show up. Eric, Mike and I had a little band meeting and said it was time for Tom to go. But we had to play it cool because we had to get our hands on the master tape.

Finally, Tom agreed to meet me at the studio because I said, "I might want to add a cowbell to one of the songs." When he showed up, I secured the tape in my possession and got up and walked out with it. I never saw Tom again.

Now that I had the master tape, we went to F's home studio, where Flash and his guitar player, Keith, mixed the tape.

***

While the tape was being mixed, we moved our rehearsals to a new location called The Rock Room. A few rock bands rented a big warehouse and transformed it into a cozy, soundproof rehearsal studio, and we were lucky enough to be a part of it.

A week later, Gold Coast Live magazine interviewed us and seemed as amazed as me at how we've suddenly become one of the area's top original bands. In the interview, she asked Mike what our music was all about, and his answer made my hair stand straight up.

He replied that we were happy the audience seemed to like our music, and he just wanted people to get up and do a little dancing.

Dancing! What the hell? I just wanted to make their eardrums bleed and tour the world! But that's what he said, and I just closed my eyes and pretended I didn't hear it.

It was right there and then that I *thought we should have talked about what we wanted the band to be projected as.* Things moved so fast from the get-go that we never sat down and talked about important things like that. Oh well, I was just happy they interviewed us.

We were also thrilled to have one of the songs, called 'Tomorrow,' play on the local rock station WSHE 105.9. They had a show at night that highlighted local up-and-coming rock bands.

I remember getting the call telling us our song would be playing that night. I told everybody I knew. When the song came on the radio, the feeling I had was equal to an astronaut blasting off to the moon.

Hoping to impress my parents so they wouldn't think they had raised such a loser, I crossed my fingers and hoped they'd tune in. I forgot where we were going, but Elaine and I heard it on the car radio when it came on. Whoa! What a thrill, my turn was coming, the Rock

Train was racing toward the bright light at the end of the tunnel, and I was going to be a rock star soon, I thought.

The next day, I stopped over at my parents' house to get their reaction. I had to hand it to them, and they sure brought me back down to earth when they shrugged their shoulders and simply said it was nice.

The next time I saw Elaine's parents, her father told me to shit or get off the pot. In other words, hurry up and become a rock star or stop trying. Elaine said her father liked me, and he just hated that his daughter was on my Rock-N-Roll Train.

Deep down, I think he was still mad at me for taking his daughter to a concert on our first date. In those days at the Hollywood Sportatorium, you could get stoned out of your head by just sitting there. The cloud of pot smoke hung in the air like a thunderstorm. When I brought her home, she opened the front door and said hello to her mom and dad, who were waiting up for her, then passed out on the living room floor. The look on her dad's face expressed a kill-the-boyfriend look, and I took off running.

***

A couple of weeks after our song aired on the radio, our new album called Rock City Road was released on cassette, and we were ready to get out and continue playing shows. It was March 17th, and Eric's 17th birthday. Still too young to legally play in clubs, but by now, we've played every club that supported the original music scene. This time, we performed at the largest club we had ever played—The Treehouse.

All excited to play, we loaded the equipment and headed to the show. The only thing I forgot to do was to check when the load-in time was. This was the well-known club that all the rockers came to. The metal-god incarnate, Rob Halford from Judas Priest, went there when he was in town.

We showed up around 7 p.m. to set up and do the sound check, but the doors were locked, and you could hear the crickets. Since it was Eric's birthday, we went out for a beer run and figured the club would be open when we returned.

We ended up drinking a case of beer in the parking lot, cursing the place for not letting us know the night was canceled and wondering where the hell the other band was. That pissed us off even more because now we thought the club told them and not us.

A few hours later, while we were busy slurring our words, cars started showing up. We found out that the place didn't open until 11 p.m. and bands didn't start until later. Oh well, it was our mistake. Now, we had to struggle to be sober on stage. We played, but I don't remember the details. One thing I remember was that I played the meanest Chuck Berry solo since we were a 3-piece band again.

A couple of weeks after that fiasco, we strolled into a place called Hawk Entertainment Studios. They wanted us to play our song called Bad Boys Are Back. It was the song we played at Roarke Hall when the riot started. We played it live about 5 times while the cameras picked up all the angles. It was supposed to be for another show on local talent, but we didn't believe it. We never heard anything about the other video we made, and probably wouldn't hear anything about this one, either.

The reason we agreed was because we had two choices: whether we could do it or not do it. By doing it, we were putting the band out there with a 50/50 chance that something good would come from it.

If we did not do it, there would be a 0/0 chance for anything to happen. This is why we never turned anything down, and you never know who'd be there watching.

It was another stepping stone, and we never turned away from anything. We were hungry. Hungry, hungry, hungry. As it turned out, nothing ever came of it.

***

Around this time, the Gold Coast Live magazine held its "Coasties" awards night at the Treehouse. The Remedy was nominated for the Best Surf Band award, which blew my mind since none of our songs referred to the beach. But it was ok, at least our name was on a list.

Full Speed Ahead

We had two recordings out and played in every possible place we could. The local rock magazine, Gold Coast Live, came out with a new issue every month, and we nearly always had something in there about us. It was time for the next step. All we had to do was find it. At this point, we probably should have been setting up little tours up the East Coast, but we were determined to get management first.

While searching for that next step, we were booked to play at the latest original music club called The Jockey Pub. It was here that our drinking got a little out of hand. Between waiting to go on stage and our newfound friends supplying us with endless drinks, it was amazing how we didn't get banned from the place.

I remember one time I was up there on that little stage, talking and toasting with the audience. I would somehow think there was a shelf behind me, take a sip from my bottle, and proceed to put it on the imaginary shelf behind me, where it would crash on the floor in front of Eric and his drums. After it happened 3 times, the owner cut me off. No more beer.

The Jockey Pub seemed to be a bad mix for us. It was near the Seminole Indian Reservation, and there were a lot of tribal ladies who came to watch us play. We'd be up there playing, and I can't explain it, but they were unnerving, maybe because they looked like Slash from Guns and Roses. They were nice enough, but they stayed in their huddle by the stage and just smiled as we played.

One time, after we finished playing, Eric jumped off the stage and ran out the front door to escape them, only to wrap his arms around a palm tree and get a splinter in his hand. When I finally met up with him, I saw his hand resting comfortably on the boobs of a tribal hottie. It seemed she had placed it there, as if on pillows, while she tried to take out the splinter.

The look on my little brother's face was priceless. Some big brother I am. I'll probably burn in hell for all the debauchery he got into at such an early age. I just walked away and tried not to laugh.

I don't know how Mike did it, but he was able to rent Roarke Hall again. Only this time, the city had security in there to make sure everything ran smoothly.

Flash had his new lineup ready, so F, The Remedy and another band rocked the hall with an all-ages Rock N Roll party. It was a great show, and everybody on the local music scene was there. Gold Coast Live magazine was on hand and gave the event good reviews in its next issue. They also printed that The Remedy doesn't let the fact that there are no clubs to play in slow them down, they go and rent a hall. Then she printed my phone number so all the interested bands who wanted to play with us could call me. That pissed me off a little, but I sure received some interesting phone messages.

At this point, I was more than ready to find management to get us to the next level, but it was harder than finding a needle in a haystack.

I also forgot to mention that when I keep doing the same thing time and time again, I get restless and bored and feel the need to move on to the next thing before I suffocate. Although I was having a blast and accomplished the impossible by singing in my very own rock group, I was suffocating.

Between the summer of '85 to the summer of '87, we played relentlessly everywhere we possibly could. New original music clubs appeared and disappeared, and we played them all. One time, we even overbooked.

We were invited to play a benefit show at the Wellaby Park Band Shelter in the city of Sunrise. I laugh every time I think about it. The city hated us for causing the riot at Roarke Hall the year before, and yet they kept asking us to play somewhere in their city.

If we were smart, we would have canceled one, but we were not rock stars yet, so we had to be seen by every eyeball that would have us. We had it timed perfectly. We would set up and play in the early afternoon, then have enough time to pack up and perform later that evening at a club called Summers on Fort Lauderdale Beach.

Of course, nothing worked out as planned. The event in the city of Sunrise started late and dragged on as people were slow to arrive. We, on the other hand, started performing at the original time and ended our show before everybody showed up to the event.

The city of Sunrise officials were mad that we were leaving before their event was over, but there was no way we were going to miss playing at Summers. The beautiful part was that there was no time listed on the contract. It just stated that we would perform at their event. Sweet revenge, I called it. Revenge for telling us we wouldn't get 1st place trophy in their Battle of the Bands.

Summers on the Beach was a huge club on Fort Lauderdale beach. So many big-name rock bands played there, from Molly Hatchet, The Troggs, Georgia Satellites, Pat Travers, Blue Oyster Cult, Iggy Pop, and so many more.

The exposure The Remedy would get performing there would be great. I thought for sure some big music biz guy would sign us for a tour around the country.

We played a good tight set to the cheers from the audience and mingled with the other bands for a while before we packed up and left. I took a big breath and carried on, believing it was another stepping stone to rock-n-roll greatness.

There was a punk rock club in one of the worst parts of Miami called Churchills. Iggy Pop played there, and many other rockers in that genre. Struggling bands like ours were required to send a demo tape, group picture, bio and references in order to get booked.

I figured out a way to bypass that stuff. We'd been around now for over a year, and in my delusional mind, I believed we were the best band in the land.

One night, I called the owner of the club and said I was the manager of The Remedy. I told him we had just finished a successful club tour in England and that I was booking a tour up the East Coast to New York. I explained the band wanted to kick off the tour in Miami and wanted to know if Churchills wanted to be the first stop.

The owner of Churchills was from England, and I thought *he'd like to see the band that had just played in his Kingdom.* I also thought *he'd ask the names of a few of the clubs we played in over there, so I looked them up.* One of them was the Marquee. Back in 1986, I had no idea that the Marquee was one of the top clubs in England; everybody from the Rolling Stones on down the line played there.

When I told him The Remedy played there, there was stunned silence on the phone for a second, and then the owner asked when my band wanted to play.

To play it off, I asked him to hold the line for a minute while I reviewed our tight schedule. When I came back on the line, I said Saturday night in 2 weeks would fit just right.

Now, there was no way a local band playing Churchills for the first time was ever booked on a Saturday night. No, you had to pay your dues and play on a Tuesday or some other day of the week when people didn't go out. If you had a good following, your band would work its way to a Saturday night spot. I couldn't believe how easy it was for us.

The weekend before we played, we stopped by the club to hand out flyers and tape them all over the walls. When we walked inside, our eyes grew twice their size, and our mouths dropped to the dirty, beer-soaked floor. There were posters all over the walls telling the patrons not to miss The Remedy next Saturday. Straight from England!

Before we could turn around and escape, there were a few guys from other bands that we had played with who came over and asked how the hell we toured England and now were booked to play Churchills on a Saturday night. We just looked at them and laughed, smacked them on the shoulder and told them that hard work pays off. When they tried to press for more information, we just pointed at our ears, letting them know we couldn't hear them talking with all the loud music, and left the building.

The night we played was great. The club was packed solid, and we played a tight show. There were a lot of people there who knew us, and before we showed up, we made up our minds not to tell anybody anything about our faux English tour or anything else. On this night, we weren't going to say anything to anybody. We were going to walk into the venue like a gang, jump on the stage, play our hearts out, and quickly disappear into the night.

I guess it worked because we had steady gigs at Churchill's for a long time. Another thing that was unheard of was that we played there a few times on a Friday or Saturday night with no other bands. There were usually at least 6 bands that would play their 45-minute set.

I remember one time when we played all night without a break. We were testing our limits and trying to impress the crew from the television show, Miami Vice.

Finally, I had to whisper in Mike's ear to do a bass solo because I had to take a leak. Mike would tell me the same, so we told Eric to do a drum solo and we'll be right back. Eric said hell no, and he also had to pee, so I stepped up to the mic and told the crowd we'd be back after a quick pee break. The crowd roared with laughter as we ran off the stage and into the restroom.

Afterward, we hung out and talked to the Miami Vice crew, and they told us Philip Michael Thomas was interested in our band. We gave them a cassette of our latest, greatest rockers and crossed our fingers. Nothing ever came of it.

The beginning of '87 started with us getting booked to play at the newest club in Miami called Banal. Believe me, it was the appropriate name for the place. It was upstairs, so we had to haul the equipment up a steep, narrow path to a long, skinny room with a tiny stage.

We never complained because we considered it a test and another stepping stone to rock stardom.

During this time of relentlessly playing at Banal, we managed to record our 3rd 10-song cassette. Again, we went to F's studio to record. Since we were a 3-piece band again, F's guitar player, Keith, played the solos. Unlike our first recording, Keith took a couple of weeks to lay down the solos.

As fate had it, the minute we were done mixing the new tape, one of the best guitar players I ever heard in my life joined the band. His name was Dave, and he always wore a Fedora like a mobster. He used to tell anybody and everybody that he was the best rock guitar player on the planet, and he'd gladly challenge anybody who doubted it.

When he told me that at his audition, I quickly listed songs like Rock n Roll by Led Zepplin, Tie Your Moher Down by Queen, and a slew of others. Without blinking an eye, his response was note-for-note spot on. Damn! We needed him in the band because two years of playing with average lead guitarists and me filling in with Chuck Berry-type solos was getting old. With this guy in the band, the sky was the limit, or so we thought.

Our new cassette, called Hot Sweaty Nights, was released about a week after Dave joined, and right away, he said he could have blown everybody's minds if he were on it. Yeah! I liked his attitude.

We continued playing Banal until one night we had had enough. We drank way too much in the crowded room that kept feeding us beer, and when we were packing up to leave, I was walking down the narrow stairs, and Mike was behind me with his amp. Suddenly, I heard Mike shouting for me to get out of the way.

I turned to see him riding his amp down the stairs with a beer bottle in his hand. Seeing no place to go, I leaped onto his amp and rode it down with him as we crashed through the entrance door and spilled out onto the street. We heard the cheers from the crowd outside as we lay there drinking our beverages, not spilling a drop.

That was the last time we ever played Banal. It was fun while it lasted, but we decided it was not the place for us anymore. We needed to play in bigger places if we were going to get anywhere.

There was a place called The Hairy Eyeball way down in Southwest Miami, out in the boonies that booked us on a Saturday night without a clue of what we sounded like. They booked us on reputation only since we were always in the local entertainment magazines.

When we finally found the place in the middle of nowhere and started unpacking, I sensed right away that this was a mistake. The crowd was a mix of rednecks and older rockers that looked like they wanted to hear Southern rock and Led Zepplin covers.

When we took the stage, I saw the questioning look on the audience's faces as we walked on with our traditional black stage attire and sleeveless shirts. Dave wore his lucky white mobster hat, which stuck out like a sore thumb, but he never played without it. Moreover, who was I to try to stop the world's best guitar player from wearing a hat?

After the first couple of songs, I knew I was right. The audience was hostile and shouted for some Led Zepplin. Since we only played original music, I obliged by telling the crowd, 'Here's a rare Zepplin song you've probably never heard," and we plowed through another one of our originals.

The nightmare continued through the entire show, and I was surprised we didn't have to fight our way out of there at the end of the night. I made a mental note to check out the clubs before we play in them in the future.

At this point, things were getting repetitive. It's no excuse, but it's probably the reason we were becoming alcoholics. Our beer consumption was way too much while playing on stage. We should have tried harder to actively seek management, but we just kept busy playing everywhere we could and hoping the right person would jump out of the audience and sign us up to be rock stars. We moved in such a blur that we didn't even take the time to find out what kind of places we were playing.

Making my mark in The Remedy

The Remedy with Tom in white Pants

Train loses a steel wheel

We continued playing all over the place like a train leading to nowhere. As was becoming standard, our latest guitar player jumped off the Rock Train. Like the song "Summer of '69" by Bryan Adams, Dave quit the band and moved to Detroit to get married.

We continued playing as a 3-piece band, unfazed at the seemingly revolving door of guitarists, and played at Churchill's again. I liked playing there because it was the place where everybody came to check out the original music scene. The crew from Miami Vice was there to see us again, and the place was packed.

Again, we were surprisingly the only band playing. Between sets, we always turned off the microphones to reduce feedback on the stage. When we were ready for another set, we simply switched the buttons on the microphones to turn them back on.

This time, we jumped back on stage and started another set, but good ol' Mike forgot to flip the "on" button on his mic. He flew into a rage when he didn't hear his vocals and threw a tantrum in front of a packed house.

Eric and I watched as he argued with the soundman and turned into a complete lunatic. It was right there and then that I knew he must have been taking something a little more potent than our usual beer.

One thing I didn't mention was that at Churchill's, we were constantly offered pretty much any kind of drug we wanted. I thought the band was always able to turn down drugs and stick to beer, but little did I know that Mike had slowly turned into a cocaine cowboy, riding high on the bullshit.

After the show, Eric and I talked and concluded that we couldn't have drugs in the band, and we knew Mike had succumbed to cocaine a long time before exploding on stage.

Five days later, before our rehearsal, we were going to give him the ultimatum to quit drugs or quit the band. To make it easier, he showed up and said he was quitting the band, getting married, and starting a family.

For a while, I felt bad and blamed myself for getting Mike into the band, where he easily fell into drugs. But then I figured he's a big boy and will follow his own path. I also felt bad because we were good friends. We followed our dreams for two years in The Remedy and had a great adventure doing it. Now, it was over. The core of the band was gone.

We auditioned bass and lead guitar players; Mike's replacement was a guy named Lenny. Our new lead guitarist was called Craig.

We rehearsed the new lineup and added cover songs so we could play four sets and perform in more clubs. I was 25 years old now, and time was getting short. We dropped the "The" and were now "REMEDY".

We played our first show at the Jockey Pub with my old band F. That night, it suddenly hit me how we had played together two years earlier. We were completely different bands. F and REMEDY had different players. The ex-players had come and gone, and now, only the strong survived. Perseverance was my new motto. It also made me wonder how many lineup changes we were going to have before we "make it or break it."

We played at the Jockey pub regularly for the next four months. It seemed like a dead end, but we made pretty good money, which we planned to save and record our next album on vinyl.

The July 4th weekend broke the monotony when we once again played at the City of Sunrise 4th of July Celebration and won the 2nd-place trophy at the Battle of the Bands competition. Even with the new line-up, the city stayed true to their word—we'd never get 1st place because of the riot we caused at Roarke Hall. Still, we couldn't care less.

Again, it dawned on me that the Roarke Hall incident was three long years ago, and we had better become rock stars soon. The highlight of that weekend was that our new friends, called ASSASSIN, won, and we had people come out on a rainy night just to see REMEDY play. What really took me by surprise, though, was seeing my dad in the crowd, standing calmly and watching next to a mosh pit.

With the new lineup, our sound was bigger and better than ever. Struggling to break out of the original music clubs and branch out to bigger clubs and audiences, it was easy to put four sets of classic covers into our sets with Lenny and Craig.

We signed a contract with a promoter called Big Beat Productions and played at a dingy hole-in-the-wall called the Plus One Club in Palm Beach. What a mistake! What we thought would be a great night of winning over Palm Beach rockin' fans turned out to be a nightmare. We played four sets to a redneck, country-music-loving crowd that hated loud music.

I remember the bartender kept crawling up to the stage and asking us to turn down another notch. We ended up turning down so low that I could hear my guitar pick clicking against my strings.

Before our last set, we agreed to screw it and blast the place. We had a contract, and they had to pay no matter what. The next day, I received a call from Big Beat Productions informing me that the contract had been terminated. Great, good riddance.

We licked our wounds and returned to the place that loved us— Churchill's in Miami. The audience reaction was great, and we felt like we were on our way. All we needed was good management.

In late July of '88, we went to F's garage studio and recorded another demo tape. This time, we only had 6 songs instead of 10 like our previous 3 recordings. The reason? Lenny had trouble recording his bass lines.

He'd mess up and insist on doing it again… and again… and again. Flash and I begged him to take a break, then he could get back to it when he felt comfortable. But that was no good. We'd do take after take, on top of mess-up after mess-up.

I thought I was going to have a heart attack. My idea of recording rock music was to keep it simple, keeping the song edgy with only a couple of takes if needed. In hindsight, that's probably why we sounded rough around the edges. But I was a fan of live one-take recordings. To me, you should know what you're doing before you waste everybody's time trying to record it. We weren't trying to record a Meatloaf masterpiece.

All in all, that's where the tension between Lenny and me began.

The following week, we were booked to play four nights at the Jockey pub. One of those nights, when we arrived early to do a sound check, the owner of the club told us we had to go on at 7 p.m. instead of 10 p.m. because the first band was going to arrive late.

What the hell?! Nobody was even at the club at that hour! Even the sun was still up! We shook our heads acknowledging his request, then took off and had dinner at a McDonald's up the road for four hours.

When we returned at 9:45, the place was packed. We hustled in the back door and waited to take the stage. The owner saw us and came charging over, ready to scream. Between arguing with Lenny about the order of the song lists and listening to him telling Craig that he had to have more flair onstage, I was in no mood to listen to the owner cry about us not playing in the daylight hours. I just stuck my hand out in front of his face and slipped on stage in time to play my part in the opening song, "Detroit Rock City" by KISS.

We should have been celebrating when a booking agency called K&M Productions booked us into a club called J&W Lounge, but I barely remember it all. I just remember Eric and I felt like we were dragging dead weight through quicksand. Instead of fighting to make it to the top, we were fighting each other about everything. After this show, we kicked Craig and Lenny out of the band.

***

It took Eric and me three months to get back in the game. We got a taste of the dark side of what happens in bands when members split in different directions and end up sabotaging the goal of making it through thick and thin.

It took another five months for us to find what we thought were the best replacements when we added Willy on bass and Andre on lead guitar.

It was now 1989. Again, something had to happen soon because I was now 26 years old. It never crossed my mind that we wouldn't make it, but…I was getting old.

In March, our 6-song demo tape "Breakaway" was released. Every time I listen to it, I think of the hell Lenny put us through recording it.

We were back in action and pretended we didn't skip a beat. The first show with the new lineup was at The Treehouse. Unlike the first time we played there, we showed up later and were greeted by the eager crowd.

After that, we continued playing the same circuit and played to a packed house at Churchill's before Willy decided to leave the band. Of all the people, Lenny returned, promising to get along and work harder for the common goal.

At this point, Eric and I weren't as picky about who was in the band. We were the core members and needed good management. We couldn't be bothered by the inner-band turmoil. If Lenny and Andre had issues, that was their problem, and we had to keep pushing to make it to the big time; I wasn't getting any younger.

With the new, improved lineup, we returned to the City of Sunrise's annual battle of the bands and the 4th of July celebration. We won our customary 2nd place trophy, but this time, the audience's reaction was insane. They loved our show, and we signed autographs! I remember looking at the city officials and laughing at how they held their promise and refused to give us 1st place in the event. It was laughable, and I didn't care. My goal was to become a rock star.

But four years of struggling to make it were killing me. We needed a good manager to take us to the next level, but it seemed impossible.

We kept plugging away and were invited to a huge outdoor party. We were to play on a big four-foot-high stage in a field with some other bands opening the show. My first thought was that we don't play at outdoor parties. We were too loud, and the police were sure to come after we strummed our first chords.

But this place looked like a mini-Woodstock. In here, everybody was part of the crowd—from bikers, punkers, and rockers to your customary drug dealers—waiting to tear it up.

My wife, Elaine, was our official photographer and walked around the grounds with Lenny's wife, snapping pictures.

As we waited to go on stage, Elaine suddenly staggered backstage and said she thought somebody had put something in her drink. She looked drugged and ready to collapse. I dropped what I was doing and held her close in my arms to see what was happening.

Apparently, some guys tried to pick them up and slipped something in their drinks. I walked her to the car, and she collapsed in the back seat. Since it was showtime, I had a couple of friends watch her until the show was over.

I was furious. To make matters worse, the band that had just got off stage was harassed by some tough guys in the crowd. They got on stage and shouted into the microphones and went stage diving, and did everything else that would cause a band to cringe.

Before we played our first song, I warned the crowd that we would kick anybody's ass who came up on stage. Well, that opened the gates of hell. We played our set while kicking faces like soccer pros and punching and destroying every idiot who tried to come up on the stage. I think I saw Andre get sucker-punched, but that was the only band casualty. My only concern was getting back to Elaine and making sure she was alright.

By the end of the year, we still needed management, and we were nowhere close to our goal of becoming rock stars.

We went back to F's studio to record another demo, hoping this would be the one to land us a management and a recording contract.

During the recording, Lenny went back to his old tricks again, forgetting his parts and dragging out the entire process. My only thoughts were that recording rock songs shouldn't be this difficult.

At this point, Lenny and I clashed over everything. We even stopped talking to each other at rehearsals, and it was hilarious. I'd call out the next song, and Lenny would lean over and ask Eric what the next song was.

Our next show was at a new club called Knobby's. The stage had mirrors all over and a giant disco ball on the ceiling, hanging over a dance floor. My first thought, of course, was that we mistakenly got booked at a disco, but we made it work when a friend worked the stage lights during our show.

It looked like disco hell as we plowed through the show with a deafening roar. Our light man had the lights flashing at lightning speed, and the disco ball looked like it was going to spin off into the crowd. We had a blast.

When it was over, I thought we'd catch hell from the club owner when he and a bouncer named "Tiny" came over to me. Tiny was a big guy full of muscle. He had a tattoo on his inner bottom lip that read "Fuck Off!" when he pulled his lip down.

They came storming over as I braced myself for a fight, but they burst out with smiles and said it was the best time they ever had. Whew! What a relief.

***

A few weeks later, Flash and his guitar player, Keith, finished mixing our new demo. It was to be called "Young and Dangerous". Unfortunately, this recording got lost in the midst of time, as tragedy struck and nearly destroyed the band.

One night after one of our shows, Lenny invited the band, wives, girlfriends, and band friends to his house for an after-party. I declined to go since we weren't getting along, which left Eric to drive alone. He had a huge Ford pickup and four-wheel drive with big tires that could win trophies at car shows.

After the party, Eric was driving home on I-95, and his tire got stuck in a groove in the road where there had been construction going on. His truck flipped and tumbled as Eric was flung out through the small back window opening. The next day, he woke up in the hospital to find a preacher standing over him, delivering his last rites.

The last thing on my mind was Remedy. I just wanted my little brother to survive. On top of that, I felt guilty for not going there with him to Lenny's party.

At this point, while Eric was in traction at the hospital, I was ready to give up music. I felt bad that two of the core members of my original band found trouble while trying to reach our dream, or should I say, my dream? I never really asked them if that was their dream. When we started, they had no clue how to play an instrument or be in a band. I just showed Mike a few chords, and Eric came along to beat on the drums.

Everything happened so fast that we never looked back or talked about what they wanted to do with their lives. Now I think that it's my fault that Mike got mixed up with cocaine, and my little brother Eric wouldn't have been in the car accident if he hadn't stopped playing baseball to play drums.

A few weeks later, it looked like Eric was going to make it, so Andre, Lenny, and I started rehearsing again with a temporary drummer.

We had a show coming up, but out of respect for Eric, I didn't want to play on stage without him. Andre and Lenny tried talking me into it, telling me the show must go on, but I really wasn't feeling it.

Suddenly, before a mutiny could transpire, Eric was out of the hospital and ready to rejoin the band. He even managed to get a date with the nurse who saw him naked.

I thanked the temporary drummer for filling in while Eric was out, and the disappointed guy walked away, never to be seen again. In hindsight, it would have been thoughtful to let him play a show with us...but the bond between brothers is stronger than my thoughtfulness. I felt bad for a minute, but then again, he's not the first guy to get screwed in the showbiz.

***

We continued playing the same clubs relentlessly. This was the stage of Remedy that became tedious. Looking back, this should have been the time when we took the leap and moved to New York or LA if we were serious enough to make it. We played the same clubs relentlessly for four years. If we had sat back to see what the problem was, we would have seen that the band was played out in South

Florida. Instead, we continued our path, waiting for management to jump out of the audience and sign us up.

89 with fan club

Train Wreck

With Eric back in the band again, we continued our assault on people's eardrums until Andre started screwing up and got himself kicked out. While auditioning lead guitar players, it suddenly occurred to me that the band wasn't much fun anymore.

When we first started, I would come to rehearsal with a new song, and we'd add the band's mojo to it, and everybody was happy. Nowadays, I'd come in with a new song, and I'd get reactions from Eric and Lenny explaining how they weren't "feeling it."

One night, on the spur of the moment, I escaped the band's lunacy and gathered the nerve to play three songs solo with my 12-string acoustic/electric guitar. There was a place in Pompano called Charcoals that had 'Talent Night.' Musicians and comedians would get a 15-minute shot on stage to do their thing, and judges filled out their scorecards to see who'd be the winner.

I couldn't have cared less about the judges, and I just wanted to get up there and see if I could play solo. I was surprised at the encouraging response I received from the audience and judges. Now, I had something to fall back on in case the band didn't make it. I was 28 years old and exploring my options.

I remember someone in the audience came up to me when I finished playing and said I looked so cool up there, sitting on a stool with my 12-string, cool boots, and dressed like Johnny Cash. I remember how relieved I felt hearing that. Up there on the stage by myself, with no band members to deal with, just me. It felt good, and I dressed the part. Other performers wore shorts and t-shirts, and some even wore flip-flops. Again, I understood that image plays a big part.

There's nothing more boring than seeing somebody on stage with normal streetwear.

***

While still slogging through auditions for lead guitar players, I got a call from a member of a popular local band. Rusty, the leader of the D.T. Martyrs and a friend of mine, told me Lenny auditioned for his band.

Well, seeing that REMEDY required 100% commitment if we were going to make it, this news was treason and grounds for firing Lenny. I couldn't wait to tell him at the next rehearsal and see his surprised reaction. Poor guy had no clue that Rusty would report his treacherous ways.

After a two-month break, we made a point to clear out the soap opera vibes and get back to the three-piece rockin' band that REMEDY was known for. We got Andre back in the band, and I returned to playing bass guitar. We quickly got booked at Churchills again to blow the roof off. The crowd's reaction was fantastic.

In dire need of a good manager and recording contract, we once again worked on our demo tape and went to a photography studio to get professional pictures taken. It was time to make it. After five years in REMEDY, I felt like we were stuck in a hole, just going through the motions.

***

We played at Knobby's again to a deafening roar and packed the place. "Tiny," the bouncer, must have been on something—he marched through the audience like a wild bull, showing off his lip tattoo to everyone he slammed into. I couldn't stop laughing.

We played our hearts out for the rest of the year. The audience reaction was good, but I was suffocating. I finally realized our Rock 'N' Roll Train had slammed head-on into a dead-end brick wall.

After eight years of the excitement of playing guitar in front of live audiences and six of those years leading my own band, I was more than grateful for everything that I had been through up to this point. But I was not a rock star yet, and I was swimming around in quicksand, doing the same shows at the same places in front of the same audience. I think my big mistake was to keep playing and hoping a good talent agent or manager would somehow appear out of nowhere and sign us up for a tour.

I didn't see it coming, but I was glad it did. Remedy played its last show at a club called the Overflow Pub. We didn't know it would be our last until we finished playing. While packing up, Andre walked up to me and said he was quitting.

His little sister was starting a band because it looked fun. She was going to be the singer and Andre was going to be her guitar player. I wished them well and never heard or saw anything from Andre again. I guess they forgot to add 'hard work' to their fun little band idea because I never heard anything from their band, either.

***

Without good management, we were just another deadbeat band on the train to nowhere. I thought it would be a hard decision, but Eric and I were more than happy to call it quits after the last show.

We couldn't bear the thought of auditioning more guitarists to keep doing the same thing over and over again. There's a thick wall between bands that can break through to the other side and bands that can't. We cracked it, but not hard enough.

I Rode The Rock Train

In hindsight, I blamed the guys in the band for not wanting to learn my newer songs, but in reality, they were probably just getting too old to continue the way they were when we first started. We were in our late twenties and pretended that we weren't falling apart at the seams. We should have kicked Lenny out a long time ago and got somebody who could contribute the way Mike did.

Instead, we were happy to go with the first bass player who liked what we were doing until the drama started, and we were relieved when we fired him for his disloyalty.

With that kind of thinking, we couldn't blame ourselves for the band's misgivings.

***

A few days after the death of Remedy, the funniest thing that crossed Eric's and my mind was not music. We were sick of it. Instead, we were going to become top-notch beach volleyball players. That's right, after wasting six years of our lives playing in a band, we were going to relax, drink beer, watch reruns of television shows we've missed out on, and become professional beach volleyball players. To this day, I still wonder what the hell was going on in my mind.

Can't Escape the Rock Train

January of 1991 marked a fresh start, but our volleyball practice was getting boring fast. Still, stepping away from music had been good for me. It made me realize just how much I missed being the lead singer in a rock 'n' roll band.

For over a decade, I did nothing but write songs, play in a band, promote, record and all the good times, bad times, and heartbreak that went along with it. I was by no means a rock star, but at least I felt special. I was an entertainer. I know it sounds hackneyed, but damn it, I entertained people, met the crazies in that world, and most of all, I wrote the songs that I played on stage. I saw how many people were entertained, and I missed it. I missed it badly. Now I just went to work every day and came home, just like ordinary people.

I felt like a surfer who wipes out on a huge wave that keeps you sucked down on the sandy bottom until you nearly drown. I couldn't breathe. I was suffocating.

I love my wife Elaine with all my heart, and she knew how unhappy I had become. I was a fish out of water. I had no choice but to do the right thing and get rockin' again. It was the only thing that kept my interest, and I truly believed that it was the only thing I was sent to planet Earth to do.

As Superman came to earth to protect people and stood for truth, justice, and the American way, I came to earth to entertain people and stood for sex, drugs, and rock n roll.

With Elaine's blessing, she kicked my miserable self in the groin and told me to get back out there, where the lights were shining on me.

Eric, too, missed playing drums and the wild times we had in the band.

That was it. We were going to get a band going again. Only this time, we had to be different. We had to stick out like a streaker on prom night.

We were at a circus one day, and as I watched the clowns, I said to my brother, "Why don't we start a band called 'klownz'? With a K and a Z… 'KLOWNZ.'"

Eric thought it was a good idea, so we thought of how we'd look. We weren't going to wear makeup like sad or happy clowns. We would have makeup like ROCK KLOWNZ! We'd make up our faces, and that would be the face we always wore. Then we thought of KISS, and it sounded like we'd be doing the same thing; we'd be a KISS wannabe rip-off. No, that wouldn't work. People would hate us, and the ridicule would be overbearing. KLOWNZ would never work; we'd be a bad joke.

But then again, clowns wore makeup, and they'd been around a lot longer than KISS. Alice Cooper once said there's always something scary about a clown. His makeup also resembled a clown.

There was a band called King Diamond that got sued by Gene Simmons because the singer wore makeup that resembled his. But tons of rock bands wore makeup throughout the midst of time, from the Rolling Stones, NY Dolls, and Twisted Sister to countless others. Even Bob Dylan wore face paint in the '70s.

All these people wore makeup to stand out from the rest of the flock and be different. They wanted to be wolves in the land of sheep.

Remedy was my favorite band to be a part of. But after trying for 5 years to make it, we failed. All in all, we were just another brick in the wall. We squeezed every ounce of energy out of Remedy until there was nothing left.

This time would be different. We were going to stick out like a beacon in a stormy sea. We weren't going to wait for the lights to come shining on us; we were going to overpower them with our floodlights!

Suddenly, it made sense, and we set out to make it happen. We'd be Rock-N-Roll KLOWNZ. The challenge of a jeering crowd would make the challenge better. We'd have to play like the best band on planet Earth or suffer the consequences.

We placed an ad in the local rock magazine for a lead/rhythm guitar player who would wear more makeup than his sister and wear clothes that you wouldn't want to be caught in walking down the street.

You can imagine how few calls we got, but one guy named Mark answered the ad and auditioned. After passing the audition with flying colors, he was all aboard with our KLOWNZ spiel.

We planned to keep it a three-piece band to add to the thrill of audiences questioning how such a great sound could come out of a three-piece band. Eric and I would provide the tight rhythm section while a great guitar player would do the rest. Mark had no problem in that area because he was one of the best players I had ever heard of. He reminded me of Andy Scott from Sweet with all the effects he used.

We rehearsed for a month and became tighter than tight. We made it a rule not to look at the fretboard while playing, and nobody wants to see a clown standing around looking down at his guitar like all the other bands. We wanted to keep eye contact with the crowd as we ran around the stage like lunatics.

We also practiced moves that we would use during our shows, almost making fun of the hair-metal bands that had become popular in recent years, only we did it with clown faces.

On February 28th, KLOWNZ was ready. We had to be ready because our very first show was a huge event in Miami Beach. It was a four-day event called 'Rock-a-Thon.' 150 rock bands were set to play in a huge rock club called Washington Square.

It was the perfect place to introduce KLOWNZ. Everybody who was anybody would be there, including every band worth their salt. This show would make or break us.

A week before the event, the 150 bands gathered at the club for a meeting. After the meeting, we were to walk a block and have a group photo on the beach for the promotional poster.

We waited until the last minute to walk into the meeting for maximum effect. As expected, heads turned from the 149 other band members and the promoter and the club staff. The laughs and taunting were hilarious, and some guys even tried to pick a fight.

Before we walked in, we reminded ourselves that this was to be expected, and we took it all in stride. If rock 'n' roll had a fraternity, we were at the hazing stage and biding our time before exploding on the scene.

Even the promoter had his little dig when he said most of us are here to play a good show, while some bands just want to rip off KISS while staring us down.

When the meeting was over, and we walked over toward the beach, we had to continually remind ourselves not to fight any of the hostile-looking band members who thought we were a joke. It was funny, I knew and played with half the bands while in Remedy, but nobody recognized me.

The surprise came when we hit the beach. As the 149 other bands took their places for the group photo, KLOWNZ was pulled away by tourists and locals who thought we were rock stars and ogled all over us.

Remember what I said about the image? Well, the image of KLOWNZ was ten times more than the other bands. We also made a point to go out of our way to be approachable. The other bands tried too hard to be cool and acted like they couldn't be bothered by the people stopping to see what was going on. Not KLOWNZ, we acted and played the part of the rock stars we were. We stood for pictures, shook hands, and gave hugs to everybody on the beach who accosted us.

As we sat on a bench with bikini-clad women on our laps taking pictures, we were interrupted by the photographer shouting over, "When you KLOWNZ are ready, come over here so we can get this picture taken." We gazed over to the group of long-haired freaky people and saw them all staring at us, and they must have been thinking, "Those sonofabitches!" Not a single person on the street stopped to talk to them, but KLOWNZ, we had a small mob hovering around.

To make matters funnier, when we finally came over for the picture, the cameraman placed us front and center. I made a mental note: This KLOWNZ idea is going to be great.

A week later, it was showtime. Our 45-minute set was scheduled for around 3 a.m. I think the bands started around 5 p.m. to 6 a.m.

We met the soundman, and luckily, he seemed to like what we were doing. We also gave him a nice tip so that he'd work the stage lights and make us sound good. Backstage and waiting to go on, we endured more harassment from the other bands but still got ready to rock.

When we hit the stage, the lights and sound were incredible. I watched the faces of the audience, and they looked completely blown away. We ripped through one song after another with perfect precision.

When we got off the stage, we were treated like conquering heroes. The bands that had mocked us were now patting our backs and telling us we sounded great. The stage crew wasn't too happy, though, because they had to clean up the mess from exploded confetti balloons and white powder residue that also exploded in the balloons to make a better effect with the lighting.

We didn't have stage names yet, but Eric got his name that night. As he bent over to tie his shoe, a lovely lady walked by and grabbed his butt and said, "And what's your name, ButtButt Cheeks?"

As he jumped up and turned around, he smiled and asked how she knew. So, from then on, Eric was known as Buttbutt Cheeks, Mark was King Thruster, and I was Izzy Rele.

We also decided never to reveal our true identities, and we were never seen without our makeup. Doing this may have sounded like ripping off KISS, but hey, Batman, Superman and a slew of other superheroes also concealed their identities.

***

Now that we had made a splash in Miami, it was time for an assault in Fort Lauderdale. We played at Knobby's with the disco ball and nearly blew it off the ceiling. The audience loved the show, and the owners hated the stage cleanup. Again, there were a few locals from the club who tried to give us a hard time, including "Tiny," who never found out Eric and I played there in REMEDY. But once the show was over, they scrambled over with their bleeding eardrums and joined our fan club.

Let me tell you about the fan club pamphlet we gave out at the shows. It had our picture on the front cover and an explanation of how KLOWNZ came to be inside. It told the story of how three musicians who had never met before went to a circus one day. As they were in the big top, a terrible lightning storm struck the tent while watching the clown show. They survived but ended up in the hospital. While there, they had a strange urge to meet and become KLOWNZ.

It was hilarious, and the audience loved it so much we almost believed it. We also made up our minds to never tell the truth about our true identities or anything else. When asked questions, we always made up the craziest stories on the fly. If anybody wanted to know what was going on in the world or anything else pertaining to reality, they wouldn't hear it from us. We were 100 percent pure fictional entertainment.

A week later, we were booked to play Washington Square again. Two bands played before us in their allotted forty-five-minute time slot. We had a one-hour show, and I was surprised they gave us the extra fifteen minutes.

When we hit the stage, we were halfway through our first song when we blew the power in the entire club. We had to wait backstage for over an hour until they fixed the problem. When we returned, we started exactly where we were in the song when the power cut off!—AGAIN. It blew everybody's mind.

Two days after that show, we were booked to play at Knobby's again.

***

As the KLOWNZ Train was picking up steam, we received an offer to open a show for a band called Bright Fire, who were having a big showcase for a record label in South Miami. Radio station WSHE, South Florida's biggest rock music station, was there for the event.

When the three of us strolled in the back door together, we were met by the female lead singer, who proceeded to shake, rattle and roll and nearly pass out. Before I could get carried away and start thinking I had the same effect on women as Elvis, we learned that she was dreadfully afraid of clowns, especially rock-n-roll KLOWNZ.

We peeked behind the curtains and looked at the stage. There were big, clear cubes all over the stage floor. Some were connected to make stairs, and others looked strategically placed. We were told that Bright Fire was going to stand on them and never actually touch the stage; they were very eccentric…and we were very eager to upstage them and explode our balloons with a never-ending supply of confetti and baby powder.

While we were plotting out our stage ascendency, their manager casually walked over and told us we could not use any of our effects, stand on the cubes or run around. In fact, he pointed at a small taped-off area in the center of the stage where he expected us just to stand and play for thirty minutes.

We shook hands and agreed, wondering who in their right mind wanted us to open for Bright Star's big event. We were KLOWNZ, and we had to put on the greatest rock show on earth!

When we hit the stage, the room was filled to the limit with radio station people, record company execs and a dumbfounded audience.

We played a loud, tight set and ran up and down the cubes like kids on a playground. The crowd and guys from the radio station loved it, but Bright Fire's manager looked like a frightened maniac as he ran up and down the front of the stage, screaming for us to stay off the cubes.

All in all, it was one of the weirdest shows we've done so far. Even though we couldn't use our exploding confetti balloons, we conquered the main attraction and left our mark for the record executives and radio stations to see and take note of.

I used to wonder about whatever happened to Bright Fire because, after the show, I never heard the name again. Maybe if they had a different opening act, things could have worked out better for them.

***

Just as quickly as we exploded on the scene, our next move caused an implosion. We somehow got a chance to record at a secret, top-of-the-line recording studio called RT60. Supposedly, it was used by Paul McCartney, but nobody there gave us complete confirmation.

The deal we had was to record a 3-song demo in one night. That included recording the basic tracks, adding guitar fill-ins and solos, lead vocals and backups, and mixing. We took the challenge.

It took half the night to try to get the drum sound we wanted. The look on Eric's face said it all. He was tired of the producer, tired of playing half the night to find a good thunderous sound, and generally sick of the entire situation.

What really pissed him off was that after all the fussing around, they ended up triggering the drums. I don't know the details of it, but the result sounded like electronic drums. For me, I just plugged my bass guitar directly into the board and got the best sound.

Around four a.m., I was tired, and my voice was scratchy when it finally came time to add vocals. By sun-up, we had the finished product and hated it. The producer made it sound polished instead of the blistering, edgy sound we thought he understood we wanted.

Mark was so miserable that he left the studio feeling like a failure, and we never got back together to talk about it. We quickly construed that in our little three-piece power band, there were two different ideas of recording. On one hand, Mark was a great guitarist and a perfectionist. He went to extremes to make sure he sounded great. On the other hand, I wanted to get in there, lay down the tracks on the first or second take and be done with it. In my mind, that is the only way to keep a simple, power-rock band honest. If we were making a symphony, it would be a whole different story, but hell, it was only rock-n-roll.

Nobody quit; we just never spoke or rehearsed again. Days turned to weeks, and weeks turned to months. Nobody picked up the phone to see what was going on, and KLOWNZ faded into history.

***

It took six months until Eric and I decided it wasn't our fault for the recording mess. There was no way a band could suddenly get an offer to record for one night and expect to sound perfect; even the Ramones couldn't pull that off. It would have been easy if it were like when we were in The Remedy and recorded the first album in a home studio in one day, but now it was different. KLOWNZ was in a professional studio with a professional producer and engineer. Eric and I were now in the company of pros who didn't know anything about the sound we wanted.

I'm not blaming anyone, but I was wrongly hoping the three of us were more like-minded than we were. Mark was clearly the better musician, but our three-piece power band was designed to incorporate the best.

Drums and bass laid down a tight rhythm section while the lead guitar was front and center. My thoughts after the disastrous recording were that Mark thought he was too good to stick around and decided to jump off the train.

We waited long enough and finally held auditions for King Thruster's replacement. After weeks of frustration, we found another guitar player who liked to wear more makeup than a woman. Surprisingly, we had quite a few auditions. We didn't say KLOWNZ was looking for a guitar player, but I guess they figured it out. A guy named Ken passed the audition and became Kenny Kinetic.

KLOWNZ

A visit from Iron Maiden

Back In Action, Full Speed Ahead

On March 6, 1992, KLOWNZ returned with a vengeance. Our first show with the new lineup was again at Washington Square's Rock-a-Thon '92.

This time, we were greeted like royalty and played our hearts out. Not wanting to be seen setting up our equipment on stage to ruin the mystique, we were fortunate to get Flash from F as our stage manager and a couple of friends helping as roadies.

When people asked about King Thruster, we said he had been kidnapped in Japan and held hostage in a woman's prison and that Kenny Kinetic was given the ability to keep KLOWNZ rolling. That was that. We gave them a bizarre answer, and they ate it up.

***

The following week, we were booked at one of the biggest and most popular clubs in South Florida called The Button South. The Kinks, Ramones, Motorhead, Skid Row, Ace Frehley, Joan Jett and a slew of other rockstars had played on that stage, and now I was…. What a thrill! It made me feel good when I met the soundman and tipped him some cash to make us sound great and he said, "Glad to see you guys are back, Izzy." Wow! We broke on the scene for five months and were gone for 6, and this professional sound man that I had never met before missed us.

A week after the fantastic Button South show, we played for 2 nights in Miami at a smaller club called The Blue Marlin Rock Club.

The place was packed both nights, and this is where we started giving out our sweaty, makeup-smeared white gloves after the show.

It was funny, and we actually had people coming up and asking for a piece of our costumes.

We were constantly playing live shows. When we weren't on a stage somewhere, we were walking into clubs dressed in our costumes, promoting ourselves. If it looked like the local rock scene papers weren't going to print something about us for their next issue, we made sure we sent some kind of bizarre story for them to print.

Everything was going great, except we lacked the two most important things: a good manager and a recording contract. The clock was ticking, and I was 29 years old!

There was a guy named Zack who owned a rock paraphernalia shop on Hollywood Boulevard (Florida) called Zack's Rock Shop. He made clothes for bands and sold metal studs and everything that went with it. Zack looked like the twin brother of Rob Halford with a shaved head and beard.

I heard he also had connections and managed a couple of bands. One afternoon, I walked into his store and started nosing around. Since I've been playing in bands for ten years and was never approached by a manager, I figured it was time to go out and get one myself blatantly. Zack seemed to fit the bill.

I told him I was in a band that needed a manager and heard he did that sort of thing. He gave me the spiel that he had already managed a band and wasn't interested in another at this time. He asked me what the name of the band was, and I told him I work for a band called KLOWNZ. He looked at me and asked, "What do you mean, work for them?"

I didn't want to tell him I was Izzy Rele because hiding our identity was part of our schtick. But he saw right through me and grinned. Cover blown. He changed his mind and said he would manage us.

He made it clear that if he managed, he called the shots. I agreed and set out to take the good news and contract to our next rehearsal, where Buttbutt Cheeks and Kenny Kinetic could sign on the dotted line.

Eric and I signed the contract without any problem, but to my amazement, Kenny wanted nothing to do with it. I explained that Zack would only book us in the big clubs. The smaller clubs would be a thing of the past. Not only that, but he had connections. I told him that without management, KLOWNZ would keep playing the same clubs and stagnate into the kind of slow death Remedy had experienced.

He wasn't having any of it. He said he was involved in lawsuits with his previous band's contract, and that was that. He was not signing. We hit that magical fork in the tracks where choices and consequences had to be made. Kenny Kinetic chose to jump off the train while the Rock Train was picking up speed.

I called Mark and told him we had a contract for him to sign with Zack, and he miraculously became King Thruster again.

I thought Zack would be a good fit for KLOWNZ because he was a bit of a showman himself. He dressed and gave himself an image that looked like P.T. Barnum meets heavy metal-biker-gang leader. He was always dressed in black and wore a biker vest full of graffiti and pins. He wore more jewelry than a pawn store showcase shelf. Just the sight of Zack and KLOWNZ walking into a club together caused a public scene. It was great.

Along with Zack, we were fortunate to have his best friend and video producer, Andrew, filming nearly every show we did. (*You can check out some of his videos on Facebook. If you search, KLOWNZ MOCK AND ROLL.*) He also hired two roadies. Since F was in another lull, Flash stayed on as lead roadie and stage manager. I had a female named Tori to set up my bass guitar gear, and King Thruster had a guy named Billy to set up his equipment while Flash set up the drums.

After the gear was on stage, the three of them would blow up the confetti-filled balloons, hang them on a 20-foot-long PVC pipe suspended from the stage ceiling, set up the fog machine and make sure everything was in working order. While all this was going on, we sat backstage and made sure no one could see us. Zack didn't want anyone to catch us wandering around the club before showtime and ruin the mystique.

All the other bands hung out with their friends at the bar until it was their turn to play.

But not KLOWNZ. We wanted the full effect of entering the room and making heads turn. We were never hanging in the club by ourselves. When we walked to the stage, we did it together. When waiting in the wings to go on, we stood together. We were always seen as a three-piece group of weirdos who landed in the club to blow your eardrums out and put on a show. It was all in the visual effect.

Looking back, I know there was no way we could have sat backstage and hid from the audience before showtime if it weren't for Flash, Tori and Billy. It would have ruined the visual effect if we were seen all over the club and setting up our gear like the other bands.

Flash and I were the best of friends, and he wanted the excitement of helping and being a part of it all. Tori was a makeup artist who worked on the sets of some well-known B-horror movies, and we were all surprised she wanted to join our rock train. Billy, on the other hand, was the kind of guy who worked carnivals. A great guy, but there was no doubt he was born to be a carnival ride operator.

I remember one night when he was starving. While we waited for our time to hit the stage, I gave him ten bucks to buy something to eat. After he ate and finished setting up the stage,

we waited in a corner until showtime. Billy was roaming around, still hungry, and spotted a half-eaten hamburger on a table. We watched with fascination as he sidled up to the table, took a quick look around, then scooped up the burger and inhaled it in one swift motion. Wow! Where do you meet these people?

At this point, it wasn't all fun and games. Zack caught me gargling with saltwater one night and felt the need to tell me I should sing from my diaphragm. He sent me off to a singing instructor once a week to keep me from damaging my throat.

My first thought was to tell him to stick it where the sun doesn't shine, but then I realized I had to give a little to take a little. I had been singing lead vocals for well over eight years and blah blah blah. Long story short, I took the lessons to satisfy the managers' whim.

Another crazy Zack story was when he called me into his office one bright, sunny Saturday afternoon to tell me he had discovered a new sound that I should incorporate into my songs. Now, I never claimed to be the greatest songwriter in the world, but I liked the songs I wrote for KLOWNZ, and I think the audience did, too.

But just to show my enthusiasm for his efforts, I strolled into his office to hear what he had. Zack plugged in a guitar and strummed a chord. He smiled at the effect coming through the amplifier and thought he invented the cat's meow.

My eyes bulged out of their sockets, and I tried hard not to burst out laughing when I asked if he'd ever heard the song "Crimson and Clover" by Tommy James and the Shondells.

I hid my shocked face when he said he hadn't heard the song. I finally told him he'd discover the tremolo effect used on the vocals of that song way back in the sixties. And just like that, I blew a perfectly good Saturday afternoon.

***

KLOWNZ returned to the club scene with new management, Long Distance Entertainment (a top-of-the-line booking agency), roadies, and the guarantee of seeing the greatest rock show on earth. It was boldly printed on our flyers and in the local rags, KLOWNZ… *The Greatest Rock Show On Earth!* And we meant every word.

We now had performance contracts that guaranteed we'd be paid a certain amount and, most importantly, perform at the designated time slot that was on the contract. Clubs had a nasty habit of bumping bands earlier or later than originally stated, but not KLOWNZ. If we didn't play at the time written on the contract, the club would be breaching the contract with a well-known booking agency and would certainly crumble.

We looked, behaved and played like rock stars and kept the band rolling on a hairline budget. It sounds small, but we were paid $150 for every 1-hour show, whereas most original bands made $50, if anything at all, for their 45-minute set.

Zack received 20%, Long Distance Entertainment received 10%, Roadies split 40%, and we were left with 30%, which we used for guitar strings, drumsticks and heads, balloons, confetti, makeup and face paint.

We played relentlessly from May to the end of the year. Zack booked us into the biggest and most well-known clubs to give the impression that we were huge.

We even opened for Marylyn Manson a couple of times and had a blast. Why they wanted us to play with them was beyond me; there couldn't be two bands on the planet that were such total opposites. One was doom and gloom, and the other was a rock-n-roll celebration.

Their audience looked like the Manson family. The first time we played with them, we thought we bombed. Our shows consisted of loud guitars and driving drums pulsating like a marathon runner while they stood and watched with no reaction on their miserable faces. But to our surprise, Marylyn Manson loved us and wanted us back. He explained that his audience always reacted that way.

***

We still needed a record deal and strived to reach that goal, but to no avail. Finally, in early November, we were invited to a showcase for some record companies with a few other bands to play a show in a Miami Beach hotel ballroom.

I never knew the details, but there were supposedly record company executives from some major labels that were going to be there.

Unfortunately, when the day arrived, the weather turned stormy, and tornado warnings were issued. Nobody was on the road as we plowed our way down to Miami. We waited backstage for hours until we received word that the music executives would not be able to make it due to the storm. Damn, I was sure this was going to be our big break.

The organizers asked the bands to play anyway. Since we were already there, we said hell no—not after our roadies had busted their asses loading and unloading equipment, setting up balloons, strobes, and all the stage gear. There was no way KLOWNZ was going to give free entertainment.

***

We always dressed in our costumes and promoted our shows a week before we played in a venue. The night IRON MAIDEN was playing in town, we had plans to promote at the club we'd be performing in the following week. Zack was friends with Iron Maiden and was given free tickets for us to come to their show and meet them. We were thrilled but declined; we had people at the club expecting to see us, and we couldn't let them down.

Zack came up with a bold plan and said that since we'd be promoting at the club around midnight, he'd have them come to the club and meet us after their show. We thought he was nuts! But we said, "Sure thing, Zack. Have IRON MAIDEN come to us after their show."

Just after midnight, we were in the club doing our promoting thing, and the front door suddenly burst open. Zack comes racing over to us and says, "They're here! They're here!"

We asked what the hell he was talking about, and he replied, "Nicko and Dave are here."

We were huge fans of Iron Maiden and couldn't believe those two came to see us, but we couldn't act like groupies and tell them we're big fans and we love their music and have their posters on our wall. No! We cleared our throats and awkwardly went out to meet them as if we were rock stars saying hello to other rock stars.

I remember when Dave Murray walked up, King Thruster shook his hand and asked what kind of guitar strings he used. It was funny as hell.

Zack made the most of it by acting as security when we re-entered the club, standing in a corner area and ordering drinks. Nicko and Dave loved the idea of KLOWNZ, and they were really funny and down to earth.

After a while, we were hanging out, joking, laughing and having a great time, nearly forgetting we were drinking with rock gods.

It also worked out great for the KLOWNZ mystique. Everybody in the club looked on with awe as they watched the guys from Iron Maiden and KLOWNZ talking and laughing like we were old friends. I could hear them thinking, *"Who are those KLOWNZ?"*

The following week, when we played, the place was packed. Thanks to Nicko and Dave for coming to visit us. People were now coming just to try to figure out who we were behind the face paint.

Next thing we know, we're scheduled to play in the Fort Lauderdale Swap Shop. These were the days when the Swap Shop was one of Florida's biggest attractions. I think it was #5, after Disney World, Universal and the rest. They claimed about 12 million visitors a year.

The Hanneford Family Circus performed three shows a day, six days a week. They also had a concert series where Willie Nelson, Three Dog Night, Paul Revere and the Raiders, KC and the Sunshine Band and many more played on a grand stage about 10 feet high in the middle of the food court. It was not a tacky-looking stage. It looked like it was built for a Las Vegas hotel, with lights and a sound system that was second to none.

Now it was our turn to play there. I got a call from Zack on a Friday night telling me we had a show at 10 a.m. the next morning. It was an election year, and there was a Rock-The-Vote concert at the Swap Shop.

I don't know how many bands played, but one of them canceled, and Zack got us to fill the gap at the last minute.

From the minute we showed up, we knew the atmospheric conditions were in our favor. The big stage, big lights, and circus vibe wouldn't have been complete if KLOWNZ didn't perform.

When we stepped out of the car, we were greeted by management, who kindly felt the need to guide us backstage, where we met and hung out with some of the circus acts. It was funny comparing face paint tips with the professional circus clown, and the other circus performers would walk by and give us a look as if thinking, *who the hell are those bozos?*

When we hit the stage, it was electrifying. We couldn't use our wireless guitar setups because of all the interference with the electronic stores inside the building, so we used regular guitars to plug in. When King Thruster and I did our Chuck Berry shuffle from one end of the huge stage to the other, my guitar chord pulled out of my amp, and Billy raced over like a speeding bullet and plugged it back in before anybody knew what happened.

When we finished, I said my usual schtick before we exited the stage, "*Thank you, we love you, goodnight!*" Everybody laughed because it was still Saturday morning.

When we got off the stage, we were immediately surrounded by greeters who loved the show and had to touch us. I always thought it was funny how people had to touch us. I'd look at their faces, and the look they returned was that they had to touch us to make sure we were real. It was the coolest thing. Like I said in the beginning, a good image is everything.

I also noticed the pissed-off look the other bands gave us, and we were stealing their thunder. They weren't allowed in the backstage circus area; they had to mingle around in the audience like lost puppies.

Andrew filmed the show, and it looked awesome. Big stage, big lights, great sound and everybody on the ground floor and 2nd floor gave us their full attention.

Zack seized on the attention we were getting and instructed Andrew to film us as we walked around, shaking hands and giving hugs. We walked outside and got free rides on the merry-go-round while Andrew filmed. Zack planned to put together a promotional film and there was no better place to do it.

The biggest highlight of that day for me was when I spotted my dad following along and taking it all in. I had no idea he came out to see us. We were treated like rock stars that day by the management of the venue, the Hanneford Family Circus crew, and the crowd that stuck like glue while we were playing. Too bad we still desperately needed that recording contract.

***

Our next big adventure was opening the show for JACKYL in West Palm Beach. JACKYL was the latest sensation, signed to Geffen Records, with two hit songs, "Down on Me" and "When Will It Rain." Their album sold over a million copies, and they were bona fide rock stars.

We hung out with them backstage and were shocked to see how they were clearly intimidated by us. They had their hair-metal band attire and looked like 1000 other bands out there. I wore black spandex with white polka-dots, a white long-sleeved silk shirt that was way too tight to button and way too short to cover my mid-section, colorful chokers and necklaces and black sneakers. Buttbutt Cheeks wore juicy-fruit colored spandex and a bright yellow, giant-beaded neckless with different colored Converse sneakers and King Thruster wore bright-red, baggy pants with cartoons printed on them, a white silky shirt with a black striped jacket with tails, and colorful scarves dangling around his waist. We also wore our traditional white gloves that we always ended up giving away to the fans. Of course, Jackyl was intimidated. They thought we were masculine aliens from another planet.

They also tried to make sure we didn't upstage them. The light man was not allowed to use all the lights. They wouldn't let the soundman play our intro tape, we couldn't use our fog machine or confetti balloons, and they left us absolutely no space on stage to move around.

We had enough room to stand one foot from the edge of the stage. Buttbutt Cheeks' bass drum was literally poking off the stage a few inches while King Thruster and I had barely enough room to stand beside the drums on either side.

Most opening acts probably would have complained about it, but not us, and we were KLOWNZ…the best rock show on earth! And we were hell-bent to prove it.

I remember as we walked to the stage, King Thruster tried to fist-bump one of the Jackyls, and the guy just turned his head. I smirked and continued to the stage like they weren't there.

Whoa! When we got on stage, the place was packed solid. I took my place in front of the microphone and laughed when I saw I was standing about 6 inches from the face of the guy in the front row.

Instead of our fog-filled stage and intro music creeping through the sound system, Buttbutt just counted off, and we tore through the set. Since we had no room to roam around the stage, we stood in place, jumping around like maniacs at every chance.

Our show was so tight and flawless. The crowd cheered so loudly that I thought the roof was going to blow off.

If, by any chance, the guy who stood 6 inches from my face is reading this, I apologize for my sweat, makeup and spit finding your face.

When the show was over, we fled backstage like conquering heroes. My only hope was that the guy who signed them was there to sign us. I was delusional.

I saw our manager, Zack, talking to some business-looking lady and walked over. I didn't engage in the conversation because these people only talked to managers, not their entertainment puppets.

Suddenly, I heard her say she booked six shows in Florida for CHEAP TRICK, and she wanted KLOWNZ to open the shows.

My heart sank. Cheap Trick was one of my all-time favorite bands, and if we toured with them, there was no doubt in my mind that we'd finally make the big time.

To my surprise, Zack turned to face her and shouted, "No way! That will never happen! Cheap Trick is on their way down, and KLOWNZ is on their way up!"

Whatever respect I had left for Zack as a manager vanished like smoke in a hurricane. I watched the lady turn and walk out the door, along with my hopes and dreams.

Three days later, after a show in the town of Davie, we were hanging out backstage when Zack tried to critique the show. Still furious about the Cheap Trick situation, we laid into him and had a heated argument. As he insisted we'd be nothing without him, I was shouting that we'd be on tour with Cheap Trick without him.

***

January '93 started off with a free concert. Since we were now paying management, a booking agency and roadies, we thought it was clear that we didn't do free shows anymore. Turns out, it was a benefit show for one of the local big-time bands whose drummer had blown his finger off at a recent show. We didn't even know the guy, but figured Zack did.

Our next show put us back on the right track when we returned to the Button South. Since we showed up before the doors opened so we could help blow up confetti-filled balloons and do a sound check, Zack thought he'd take the opportunity to show King Thruster and me how to get on our knees and play from the edge of the stage to the crowd's delight.

We watched as he pretended to have a guitar in his hand and pranced to the edge of the stage. When the poor guy tried to get down on his knees, he tripped and fell off the four-foot-high stage and splatted on the floor.

Thruster and I did the exact same thing and landed next to him. When we got up, we said it was a good idea, but we might hurt somebody if we fell on them. Flash, Billy, Tori, the soundman and a few others in the venue burst out laughing, which pissed off Zack.

Pissing off, our manager continued at our next show. The schedule was tight, and we barely had enough time to get our stage show ready.

The last thing we had to do was put the confetti in the balloons, blow them up and hang them on the pole that would connect to the ceiling. We all helped get things ready since our newest roadie, in charge of the balloons, failed to do his only simple task. I asked why the balloons weren't ready, and he looked up at me and whined that he had trouble blowing up balloons. Again, where did we find these people?

Then I looked over and spotted Zack writing on the balloons with a black marker. When I asked what he was writing, he flipped the balloon around for all to see and said, "I'm writing KLOWNZ on the balloons," with a shit-eating grin. Again, we all burst out laughing as all the balloons read 'KLONZ.'

At showtime, we made sure to pop all the balloons quickly so the audience wouldn't think we were a band of illiterates.

We also finished a 4-song recording around this time called 4-Play. When we gave it to Zack to shop around, he threw it in the trash and said he didn't like it.

I reminded him that just one short year ago, things worked like a charm when we took care of the music and stage show, and he managed the bookings and pushed to get us to the next level. We knew the songs were good. Zack had no idea what was good or bad.

Our last show with Zack aboard was at a place called McFly's. The owner was an ex-rocker who played with Thin Lizzy at some time or other and liked our shows but hated the mess we left behind on the stage.

By now, our stage consisted of large confetti-filled balloons with baby powder thrown in for effect, hanging from the ceiling with a PVC pole, silly string that we squirted all over us, the stage and the audience, a fog machine and two huge light boxes for King Thruster and me to stand on. There were two buttons on these that we stepped on to operate. One button was a strobe light, and the other was a bright white beaming light. These lights would go on straight up from where we stood, causing a smoke-filled KLOWNZ silhouette-from-hell stage effect. It was fantastic, and it was Flash's genius idea to build them for us.

The show was a success, but backstage was another story. We had already decided to let Zack go, and we just kept procrastinating. But when he walked up to give us another one of his misleading speeches, we let him have it. We said he was fired, and he said we couldn't do that because he quit.

A couple of days later, I was summoned to Zack's Rock Shop. I remained cordial throughout the meeting and let him say what he had to say. When it was my turn to air my grievances toward him, I told him he was great at getting the ball rolling. But when we were at a certain point, it became repetitive, and we lost faith in him to get us to the next level. I told him that when he decided we wouldn't play with Cheap Trick and I couldn't say a word about it, I was done with him. If I were doing the booking, we would have opened for the Tricksters and would have blown the lid wide open.

Years later, his buddy Andrew, who filmed all our shows, told me Zack also turned down an offer from Marylyn Manson's management to tour with them. I wonder how many other missed opportunities we had.

We carried on with me booking the shows. Luckily, it was easy since we had a reputation. Our first show without Zack was at the huge club in Miami Beach, Washington Square.

At this show, I remember we played so loud, we thought the soundman had a hearing problem. Days later, I was told by some people who attended the show that their ears had been ringing for days.

We were booked to play the Button South again, but were unable to promote the weekend before because Motorhead was booked.

Eric and I went to the show and were front and center on the stage. When Motorhead came on, a mosh pit suddenly appeared behind us. The moshers were slamming us left and right and slamming into Eric's injured back.

Three long years after his accident, his back was still recovering. The moshers refused to heed our warning, and all hell broke loose. Eric and I turned and had our backs against the stage and fought the moshers. I remember Lemmy looking down at us with a surprised look and grinning while singing 'Ace of Spades.'

When all was said and done, we were thrown out of the venue and were told never to return. Funny thing, the next Saturday night, I was dressed as Izzy Rele, sitting in the very same person's office who kicked us out, collecting money after our show. I wanted to tell him so badly who I was; I could taste it.

We continued our relentless shows throughout the rest of the year, hoping we'd finally get signed to a record deal.

***

Things were looking good as the Florida rock magazine called JAM printed our story, complete with live pictures. We always had some sort of write-up in this monthly magazine, but this time it was a full story. We thought we were finally on our way.

Two months after *The Jam magazine's* exposure, we were interviewed in XS magazine.

The Sun-Sentinel newspaper had a pullout section that listed all the entertainment happenings in South Florida, and they wanted to interview KLOWNZ, where we rehearsed.

With all our craziness, we told the interviewer we'd be happy to do it. The only thing was that nobody knew our true identities or where we rehearsed.

To our surprise, the interviewer agreed to be blindfolded and taken to our hideout. On the night this took place, we spent an hour putting on our KLOWNZ gear and climbed in the van to pick up Adam, the interviewer.

We were amazed to see him standing at the corner where we agreed to meet. To make things a little more dramatic, we sped around the corner and skidded to a stop. The van doors burst open, and we jumped out and told Adam to get into the van. Anybody watching on the busy street would have sworn the poor guy was being kidnapped by spandex-clad clowns from hell.

We explained how, for his own safety, he would need to be blindfolded because nobody who came to our rehearsal studio has lived to talk about it. He agreed, which surprised us even more. With his blindfold firmly in place, we proceeded to drive all over town, sometimes just going around blocks for a half-hour before we parked at our rehearsal place. We took him out of the van and ushered him inside and closed the door before we took his blindfold off.

I saw the look in his eyes and knew he was having a blast. He looked around the studio the same way the Penguin looked at the Batcave when he made it inside in the old Batman series.

He interviewed us for nearly an hour, and since he was such a good sport, we blew his ears off when he asked if we could play a few songs.

When finished, Adam was blindfolded again and returned to the street corner, where we picked him up.

A couple of weeks passed before we got the call to come over to the Sun-Sentinel building to have a photo shoot for the front cover. This was even funnier than when we kidnapped the interviewer.

We showed up at the building downtown and entered the private underground garage around 10 p.m. and were stopped by security at the gate. There we were, decked out in our KLOWNZ attire, wondering if the guy was going to shoot us. To our amazement, the security guy smiled, opened the gate and waved us through. Once inside, we spotted Adam and another man standing around waiting and showed us where to park.

Adam introduced us (but as I'm writing this, I forgot who he was) and escorted us into the building and into the photo studio, where we hammed it up and got some pictures taken for the XS magazine cover.

When finished, we got a guided tour of the building and press room, where we shook hands with the pressmen and smeared makeup on the few ladies who wanted a peck on the cheek.

***

We continued the same pattern of playing live and relentlessly promoting for the rest of the year.

One night, while walking down Collins Avenue on Miami Beach promoting upcoming shows, we were asked by a nightclub owner to walk through his club to energize his customers. It was a dance club, and any other hard rock band in town would have balked if asked, but we were KLOWNZ, and we were completely shameless as we were more than happy to walk around the dance floor, passing out flyers, posing for pictures and giving hugs and kisses to the dancing queens.

Derailed

The beginning of the next year started out the same as the last year. At this point, we had the music, great stage appearance, good press, and a decent audience. A record deal was still eluding us, and now it was time to make it or break it. It had been a year since we recorded a four-song demo at our home studio, and it went nowhere. We had to record a professional-sounding recording that would be taken more seriously.

On January 22nd, we began recording at Outline Studios in Miami. From the start, I knew it was going to be a long, drawn-out process.

My idea of how a rock band should record is simple: Get a good sound, record the song in one or two takes to keep the edge, then get a good-sounding mix and don't touch the knobs unless you are a band like Electric Light Orchestra or Pink Floyd.

But, of course, not everybody in a band sees things the same way. I could write another book on this recording nightmare, but it would be too boring.

Of course, we didn't want to make the same mistake as last time with Mark, so we let him pick the studio and pretty much run the show. We had nothing to lose but our sanity.

I'll just say that one thing that drove me crazy was the engineer. It took him hours to get a good mix that we could all agree on for a single song, and then, instead of leaving it well enough alone, he'd mess up the knobs and start from scratch on the second song instead of tweaking where needed. We had six songs, and I thought I was going to have to kill somebody. After all, we were a simple, hard rock band that didn't require every single song to get the treatment of a Pink Floyd album.

I remember Eric hitting the same symbol all afternoon as the engineer tried to squeeze the best sound out of it. Another time, I was upstairs in the rec room shooting pool with Flash when I decided to stroll downstairs to see what the latest holdup was. Mark is a fantastic musician, and I like to give credit where it's due, but when I walked in and saw Mark sitting on a stool with his acoustic guitar and a giant mirror in front of him, I thought I was going to lose it.

Mark casually turned to me and explained that playing the acoustic guitar in front of a mirror brings out the best quality sound.

In stunned silence, I just shook my head and pondered why a band that sounded like a mix between AC/DC and the Ramones required the pleasant sounds of acoustic guitar in the mix. If you're looking for it, you can just hear it buried in the song.

The following month, we were booked to play in downtown Orlando at a huge club called Sunset Strip. The venue was owned by Jani Lane, the lead singer from Warrant.

I heard it was impossible to get booked in there without submitting a group bio, so I was surprised when I called to book KLOWNZ, and the booking agent replied, "Absolutely. When would they like to play?"

We were booked to play on a Thursday evening, and it was supposed to be another top-notch show. The only problem was that we didn't promote the weekend before like we usually did. I don't know if it was because it was too far away or if we were just getting lazy. We sent flyers to the club instead and expected them to promote us. As it turned out, there were very few people in the audience.

You never see it coming, and you always wonder how bands just suddenly break up. Well, I didn't see it coming, but I was feeling it. It started when I was writing new songs for our recording. I never set out to be the main songwriter or singer, and it just happened that way. With both The Remedy and Klownz, I encouraged everybody to be equals. Turns out, in Remedy, we only had one song in our recordings that was written by someone other than me, but Lenny and a couple of others sang lead on a couple of cover songs when we played live. Mark wrote a couple of songs for Klownz and sang the middle part in one, and that was it.

So, while I was presenting some new songs to the band, I was all of a sudden hearing things like, "I'm not feeling it" and "The chords don't flow in that pattern." It became such a hassle to learn new songs that we kept playing the same songs in the set, and our shows never changed.

Since we were still recording in Miami, we didn't have time to promote our show in Orlando, or should I say some of us were getting too lazy to go promote in the club the week before, as what we usually did. There weren't even flyers on the walls saying we were coming. The lack of promotion resulted in only a small audience that came to see us, and I knew it set morale to a dangerously low level.

To make matters worse, our next show was at the Zipperhead Room in our hometown. We promoted heavily and were expecting to have a packed house on the night we played. Three days before showtime, I received a call from the club owner. He said he wasn't sure if the club's P. A system would be there for us on Saturday night when we play.

We weren't like the other bands that could just show up and play or not play. We had a stage show to set up and a crew to depend on.

We couldn't just walk into a club, plug in our amps, and play or not play. It took us a bit longer to set up the strobe lights, confetti-filled balloons, and the rest. On top of that, it took us an hour to get into our KLOWNZ makeup and costumes. It was too much work without knowing if we were playing or not until the last minute.

I told the club manager that if they didn't have a P.A. in the club by Friday night, we would have to cancel the show for Saturday. We had three roadies working with us who would be pissed off if they showed up and got things loaded, unloaded, set up, broken down, loaded up again and unloaded all the equipment for nothing.

When the club manager threatened that if we canceled, we would never play there again, my reply was, "We never did play there and never will."

Well, that went well.

Our next show at the Plus Five was also canceled. I don't even remember what happened there, but I believe that King Thruster couldn't make it.

The next show we played was at a club called The Cellblock in Pompano Beach. I felt like I was in a cellblock on stage. It felt like the band was just going through the motions, playing the same set list that we've been playing since we started the band.

The highlight of my evening was when my best friend and confidant, Flash, told me backstage that he thought it was great that KLOWNZ was rolling again because he missed how good the shows were.

That, coming from the guy who showed me how to be in a band and risked his neck getting me in F, made me feel like king of the nighttime world.

All in all, I think that after three years of trying to get Klownz a record deal, it finally burned a member or two out.

Six months after we started the recording of our 6-song demo, it just sat collecting dust in a box stored in our rehearsal studio.

Like I said, you never see it coming. One minute, we're working like hell to become rock stars, and the next minute, it's over. Nobody shows up to practice.

***

After three months of waiting around to see if KLOWNZ had any spark left, I had written twelve new songs that I wanted to record. My brother Eric was going to play drums, and I invited Flash to play bass. I planned to play rhythm and acoustic guitars, but I wasn't about to try solos. I kept in touch with our former KLOWNZ guitar player and gave Ken a call to see if he wanted to play.

My original idea was just to have my friends help me record my new songs, but after a few rehearsals, we had so much fun that we decided to become a band. F was on hiatus again, so Flash was all in, and Ken wasn't doing anything at all, so he was happy to start a band. Eric and I had doubts that KLOWNZ would ever play again, so we had nothing to lose.

Since we were going to be a band, I suggested that Flash and Ken should add a couple of their songs to the new recording to make everybody happy and make it feel like one of those cool bands where everybody wrote and sang songs.

While we were rehearsing with the new band, we kept things open with KLOWNZ. We weren't officially broken up; we were just going to play it out and see what Mark was going to do. Long Distance Entertainment wasn't happy with KLOWNZ, as the band turned down another show in West Palm Beach. Mark couldn't make the show because he had gotten a night job somewhere.

That was the last nail in the coffin, and I took the opportunity to tell our booking agent that KLOWNZ had broken up and I had a new band called Easy Access.

Easy Access's first show was at a popular club called Rosebuds. The audience reaction was good and we finished off the year recording a new album with the new band. I remember thinking, *This better be the band that makes me a rock star...because I'm now reaching 32 in a few months.*

We got word that Zack, our manager from KLOWNZ, had cut himself while mowing his lawn. Against his wife's wishes to see a doctor, he refused to go and ended up dying from gangrene.

On January 15th, 1995, Easy Access played with a slew of other bands for a benefit show for Zack. Nicko McBrain from Iron Maiden was also on the bill, and I was thrilled that he remembered KLOWNZ from three years earlier. He sat with us, and we laughed, talked, and drank like it was a family reunion. I had to pinch myself to make sure I wasn't dreaming.

Rehearsing with Easy Access was a lot of fun. Nobody threw any tantrum or acted like they were superior or any of that crap. We all got along just fine. I don't know, but I think that may have been the problem.

I think a little tension and hostility are the secret ingredients for the success of a rock band. When everything is blissful, believe it or not, I think it gets boring after a while. And sure enough, it did. I could only remember one rehearsal when we thought we'd get killed by a bandmate.

We were rehearsing for the next show, and Ken suddenly opened his guitar case and pulled out a gun. He didn't say anything as we stood speechless, waiting to see what would happen next. After making sure we all saw it, he calmly put it back in his case and closed the lid.

"What the hell is that?" we asked.

"Oh, it's just my gun. I keep it for protection."

Go figure. Soon after that, it seemed that Easy Access had run its course. Flash told me it was time to get back to F, which I understood completely. He lived and breathed F, and he is F. To this day, he's still F, and I couldn't be more proud of him.

I had forgotten if Ken had other plans, but Eric and I decided we shouldn't stick around with a band-rehearsing-gun-slinger, so we disbanded. I was 32 years old anyway and was pretty sure my good rockin' deeds would be filed in the "Where is he now" folder.

***

As I prepared to quit my rock star dreams and join the everyday world of humdrum life, I picked up my ringing phone, and it was none other than Mark! He wants to get Klownz going again!

My first response was…. YES! Let's get it going! I suppose I should have been a little mad that he quit, and we lost a whole year of momentum, but that's what it is, and that was then; this is now.

Besides, after about a week of being in humdrum land, I had no idea how I was going to survive without recording my songs or looking forward to the next show.

I never really thought about it, but I spent half my life recording and playing in a rock band. As stupid as it sounds, that's all I knew and wanted to do. I've missed so many other opportunities in my life because all I wanted to do was become a rock star. So, hell, yes! You better believe I'm ready to get the band going again.

We rehearsed our show for two months before we wound up playing in a bar inside a bowling alley. I know what you're thinking…a bowling alley? We checked it out before we booked it, and it was good. It was a good-sized bar with a big stage standing 4 feet high. It had a lighting system that rivaled the bigger clubs we had played in, and it was the new place where original music bands played. Gone were the times when we had management, a booking agency and roadies. Even Flash was busy with his latest F lineup.

Lucky for us, the show was a success, and Long-Distance entertainment was back onboard, keeping us busy playing for the next few months. We even had the press writing things about us again. Jam magazine printed our picture and wrote a cool article saying KLOWNZ is still alive, and you can expect their new 6-song EP called "Grin and Rear it" soon. Yes, the rock-n-roll train was oiled and rolling along smoothly for the rest of the year.

***

I will never forget one of our shows at the same club where the guys from Iron Maiden came to see us in when I strolled up to the bar to get my customary two Heinekens to take to the stage. The guy sitting next to me as I stood waiting suddenly looked at me and said, "Hey, Izzy, good luck tonight."

When I looked down to shake his hand, I was startled. Before I could say anything, he said, "Yeah, I used to work for a band that also wore makeup."

Yes, it was the big guy with the cool mustache who graced the pages in all my old KISS magazines. It was none other than Big John Harte, the #1 KISS bodyguard from the '70s and early '80s.

Wow! I was thrilled. When he told me *the boys wanted me to check you guys out,* I was speechless. What an unbelievable honor for him to tell me that Gene Simmons and Paul Stanley requested that he come to our show to check us out.

***

At the start of '96, we were frustrated that we still didn't have a recording contract. Our shows were packed. We had a fan base and a load of good original songs, and still no recording contract.

Grunge bands were all the rage now, and we decided to ditch the KLOWNZ show and carry on like a regular band. It became too much of a spectacle to do our show, while the newest trend was to look like roadies on stage. Billy and Tori departed the insanity two years earlier, and besides getting a little help here and there, it just became a flat-out pain in the ass to keep Klownz going.

It was much easier for us to just show up with our guitars, amplifiers and drums and just set them up ourselves. It was the grunge thing to do.

We were booked at a place called The Monkey Bar on Fort Lauderdale Beach, located on the ground floor of a giant hotel. Long-

Distance booked us as KLOWNZ even though we told them we changed our name to RUKKUS.

It wasn't very good. Most of the people showed up to see KLOWNZ, but they got RUKKUS instead. It was rough, and to make sure we didn't hear any whining, we cranked up to 11.

I truly believe that we were so pissed off that we tried to blow out the windows of the hotel with a deafening sound. The bartender was taking complaints from guests on the 15th floor. I took it as a symbolic end of my rock-n-roll fantasy.

Daddy's a Rock-N-Roller

As life carried on, Elaine got pregnant, and now was a good time for me to grow up and be a good dad. I was 33 years old and had failed to become a rock star. I was fine with it because when my son Brad was born, there was nothing on earth that was better than me being his father. A little shy of two years later, we were blessed with an angel and named her Angela. We were thrilled to death, and I couldn't have cared less about rockin' my life away…I was a Dad to two of the coolest little people on earth!

When the kids were old enough to walk, Elaine and I took them everywhere with us— even to our favorite restaurant/bar on Thursday nights. The kids were so cute and good that we let our bartender friends take them behind the bar so they could see what it was like. Have you ever seen little kids pouring a beer in a bar? Priceless!

Being that they were 4 and 2 years old at the time drew some frowns, but we didn't care. The frowners had babysitters and left their kids at home. They called it "Date Night." We took our kids with us and called it "Family Outings."

I think we did the right thing because even to this day, the kids and their girlfriends and boyfriends hang out with us all the time, while the couples that never hung out and took their kids out to dinner are now old and lonely because the kids rarely visit.

During these years of family bliss, I couldn't help but feel the struggle of not rockin' in a band. Can you believe it? I'm 37 years old with a great family, and I feel like a fish out of water because I'm not playing music.

I Rode The Rock Train

***

It was March 2000— the turn of the century and the return of what I do best…Rock-N-Roll.

I'm not sure, and it has never been proven, but we may have influenced my two favorite bands in the world, Cheap Trick and KISS. Let me explain before you think my ego has climbed the highest mountain.

After our manager Zack turned down the offer for us to tour with Cheap Trick, their very next album was 'Woke Up with a Monster.' I'm pretty sure it's the first album cover that didn't feature their picture on the front cover. Instead, there was a picture of a clown with a scantily clad woman.

As for KISS, well, when Big John said *'the boys' sent me here to check you guys out*, I nearly passed out. The funny thing is, the next thing we see is KISS wearing their makeup again. Of course, these two things might be coincidences, but in my mind, it was the rock gods telling me that KLOWNZ had given two of the best bands in the land a kick in the crotch— and we needed to return.

Eric and I jumped back on the Rock Train and got KLOWNZ rolling again. We found a guitar player named John who was willing to put on more makeup than a Las Vegas hooker on a Saturday night.

We rehearsed the show four months before we were ready. The reason? John was lazy and probably not the greatest guitarist we needed. With KLOWNZ, you had to get up on that stage and run around all over with a mug on your face like you were the best of the best. We had synchronized moves and confetti balloons that required popping with hidden thumbtacks taped on our white gloves. It was clearly not possible for him to do those things and play at the same time.

On top of that, I kid you not, he insisted his stage name would be Mr. Chicken. So, there we had it: Izzy Rele, Buttbutt Cheeks, and Mr. Chicken…KLOWNZ!

I remember the first time my son saw me as Izzy Rele in full uniform. It was a promotion night, and we got ready at the rehearsal studio in my backyard. When I finished, I walked through the house to get something and walked past my son, who was sitting on the couch watching television. At first, I heard a slight snicker, but when I turned to look at him, it turned into a whole-hearted burst of uncontrollable laughter, with just a speck of caution that a kid would give a six-foot clown in tights.

Our first show was at a small club in Hollywood called The Hole. We didn't have help setting up the stage, but we managed. The place was packed, and the audience loved it.

We didn't have Long Distance Entertainment booking us anymore after the hotel bar incident four years earlier, so our next show was a month later at The Hole again. I was hoping Mr. Chicken would get better with time, but he got lazier. One of the good things that came out of playing at The Hole was that there was a promoter from Peru who loved our show and wanted us to play at a huge outdoor summer music festival in Lima, Peru.

We had three months to get passports. That was all we needed—passports. The promoter was paying all the expenses; we just had to get our passports. Do you think Mr. Chicken got his? No.

His excuse was that he had no car to get anywhere, so I made plans to go pick him up at his house and get his passport taken care of.

I came over just before noon on the planned day and banged on his door. No answer. I pounded on his windows. No answer. I tried calling his phone dozens of times and got no answer. I was livid. My first thought was to call King Thruster, but too much time had gone by since we last spoke.

Later that day, Mr. Chicken called and apologized for oversleeping. My response was to take a taxi or bus and get his freakin' passport.

Even though it felt like the band was running with one flat tire, things were looking good. Our next show was at The Culture Room. This was a popular club where famous rock stars had played.

At this point, we didn't have roadies anymore, so we showed up without our KLOWNZ makeup and set up our own stage, then went backstage to put the makeup on.

I'll never forget the heartwarming compliment I received when I walked over to the soundman to pay him off to make sure he did a good job for KLOWNZ. I was without the makeup and told him I worked with the band. His response was that he was happy to work with professionals again. He said this before he knew I was paying him, and it made me feel like it was all worth it.

We blew the doors off at The Culture Room, and they had us play again two weeks later. It looked like we were back to where we left off four years earlier, but it just didn't feel right. There was no chemistry in the band with Mr. Chicken in it. He was a good guy and fun to be around, but the more we continued playing shows, the more I found out that he wasn't such a great guitar player.

Who was I to be a critic? I remember the first time I auditioned for CHAOS when I didn't know how to play three chords. But that was then, and this was now. I've come a long way since then. Klownz was built as a three-piece band. The bass and drums had to be super tight, and the guitar player had to be exceptionally good to make it work. Kenny Kinetic and King Thruster fit the band perfectly, but Mr. Chicken? Not so much.

Unfortunately, the promoter from Peru thought the same. If he had come to me about his concerns with Mr. Chicken, I would have called Mark to tell him KLOWNZ was playing an outdoor festival in the summer, all expenses paid, and I'm sure he would have been back in the band in a heartbeat. But instead, he took Mr. Chicken aside and explained kindly that his guitar solos all sounded the same.

Now, that's not the thing to say to lead guitar players who are legends in their own minds, but as it turned out, Mr. Chicken threatened to kill the promoter, and while a screaming match ensued, the end result was that KLOWNZ would not be going to Peru for a summer rock festival in Lima that would have thousands in attendance.

That was the straw that broke the camel's back, so to speak. There it was. Another rocket to propel me to become a rock star was quickly blown out of the sky. I was pissed.

After another brainstorming evaluation of what to do next, we decided to ditch the KLOWNZ show and just be another band in a world of millions. I was 37 years old and stopped fooling myself that I would become a rock star. I was a family man with a wife and two of the greatest kids on the planet, so why the hell was I still playing in a band?

The quick answer: I was a delusional idiot. But in reality— my reality anyway, it was the only thing I ever wanted to do. It was all I did since I was a teenager. It's like I had tunnel vision my entire life while still functioning through a marriage and a wonderful family. I truly believed I was put on this earth to entertain the masses, and there was no other way for me to survive without being a rock star.

We stripped down the stage show and changed our name to Slip Friction. For the next ten months, we played out in small bars and places that meant nothing to anybody. We were just a band making noise while patrons played pool and threw darts. I was suffocating.

I finally took stock of our situation and concluded that we were spinning our wheels in quicksand. Slip Friction quickly fell into oblivion, and I couldn't be happier to get out of that band's dreadful situation. It was over; I was 38 years old, and my rock 'n' roll dream had crashed into a brick wall.

***

The kids were at the age where they could participate in sports, and I stayed busy coaching and cheering them on. I convinced myself that I could live happily ever after by being the best husband and father I could be.

The sad thing was that every time we went out someplace where a local band or performer played, I burned inside and fought the urge to get back on stage.

In 2003, two years after trying to convince myself I could live without playing music, I had a beautiful 12-string, electric/acoustic Ovation guitar and 50 classic songs (that I could play without the help of a notebook or some stupid iPad attached to my mic stand) in my possession.

I started playing everywhere— little bars, a sidewalk café, private parties and anywhere people would have me. It felt good to be playing and the kicker was that I was by myself: no band members, no attitudes, no enormous equipment to load in…just me.

***

The problem was that after a while, I got bored. Where I was used to the audience gawking at me in a blistering loud rock band, I was now playing acoustic guitar to people seated at tables, conversing with each other, some with their backs toward me. I was dying, and it was a slow death.

Lucky for me, my friend Flash from F called and asked me to fill in on bass guitar for F until they could find a replacement for their Bassman, who had just flown the coup. I was back! And to make this reunion better, my brother Eric was already in the band playing drums.

I was no longer the singer in a band, but it was good to be rocking again with my buddies.

Flash won't say it, but there was something different with the signature timing of F songs and KLOWNZ songs that made me screw up ques in the setlist. When I made a mistake, I would cringe and look over at Flash for his reaction. He never reacted, being the good pal that he was, but I know it must have driven him crazy.

F had just completed a new album before I stepped in, and we were playing all over the place for the next 10 months to support it. The last show we did was at Churchill's in June of 2004. Eric and I walked into the club and saw posters of F all over the walls. I don't know why, but it drove me crazy to see that only Flash was on the posters.

I always knew that he was F, but I tried to ignore it and treat it like we were a band, not Flash with a backup band. But that's what it was. Flash is F, and that's that. You don't like it? Too bad. This was the reason I quit F twenty-two 22 years earlier. I didn't want to be in a backup band. I saw it happening then, and now the posters confirm it.

I don't remember how I acted that night, but Flash must have seen it. A week after the show, he called and told me the band broke up. A month later, F was playing without Eric and me in the band.

That's the problem you have when you're in a band with your best buddy. You don't want to hurt feelings, so you just say the band broke up and move on.

I understood completely, and we knew each other so well we didn't have to talk about it. It wasn't possible for me to be in a backup band, and he wasn't about to share F with the band. He wrote the songs and made the decisions; it was all him. He was F and still is to this day, and I'm his biggest fan.

I turned 42 years old in '05 and was busy coaching the kids in sports. I had a blast doing it and wouldn't trade it for anything, but I couldn't stop the constant urge to play live music on a stage. I grabbed my 12-stringer and went out to set the world on fire.

At this point, my dream of being a rock star was history. I just went out to play on a stage because that was what I did. For me to sustain life on this planet, I had to perform in front of an audience. There was nothing better than a live performance. Anything could happen. It could go smooth as butter on toast or as rough as licking a cactus. It was the challenge of trying to entertain. It's in my blood, and I wasn't going to get a transfusion.

I played out for the next couple of years and made pretty good money doing it. I even played at a baby shower and received $500 for my services. Wow! I should have been happy, but I was getting bored again. There's only so much you can do with people in the audience holding conversations at the table with their backs toward you.

My last acoustic show was at a place called the Sour Apple Saloon on Hollywood Boulevard (Florida). I played on the sidewalk patio, where they had tables and chairs outside. My first set started at 6 p.m., and there was hardly anybody there. I told myself it was because people just got out of work and were getting ready to go out.

My second set was better. The place was filling up, and I was getting good feedback from the crowd. My third set was feeling monotonous.

While playing, I was thinking to myself, *What the hell am I doing here?* I was missing the audience gawking and jumping around like lunatics, and all the running and jumping around I did while trying to make it back to the microphone on time. Now I was just standing there…singing and strumming on a sidewalk.

But I must say, it did sound good. My 12-string acoustic was always plugged directly into the PA system board. No effects or anything—just raw 12-string strumming through the oversized speakers, the same PA system we used in The Remedy.

My fourth set made me realize I wasn't the Jimmy Buffett type. The 45-minute set seemed to last a lifetime.

The only entertainment I got out of it was when an old lady walked up to me with a mean look and told me I was not Barry Gibb.

I couldn't help it. I burst out laughing and told her I wasn't Paul McCartney, Jimmy Buffett, Cat Stevens, or any of the other singers whose songs I was playing either.

It must have been the look on my face, but after I said that, the entire crowd laughed at the poor old lady as she scampered down the sidewalk.

When the set was over, I couldn't get out of there fast enough. I was paid $120 and spent it drinking with the patrons. I declined offers to play some backyard events and drove off into the night. It was the last time I played solo.

***

Fast forward to 2008. It's been two years since I played live. I was fine with it because I was still having a blast supporting and coaching the kids' sports.

Believe it or not, I was 45 years old and still felt the hunger pangs to play music. Lucky for me, F signed with a small record label and had an old picture of me in the band from 1982 on the front and back cover. It was an EP vinyl record called Four from '84. I wasn't in the band in 1984, but what the hell.

Flash asked me to come back into the band, and I jumped in before he could finish asking.

This time was going to be good. I wasn't in charge of anything or had any illusions about becoming a rock star. I was just fine to be the bass player backing Flash, and I could be content being in F for the rest of my life. The only thing I had to do was play my parts tight.

Tight was the problem. Rehearsals went fine, but playing live was a mess. The drummer and I stayed on the mark, but I could never hear where the guitar player was or what he was playing. It was a mess. Every time the poor guy plugged in his guitar, he never had the same sound. During rehearsals, we waited patiently for him to find a coherent sound, but the sound he had on stage reminded me of a screeching steel wheel from a freight train. But the F fans loved him, and I figured it was the only reason he was in the band.

I had nothing against him. In fact, we had a great time traveling. I remember one night in Tampa when we were back in the hotel room. We were on the second floor, sitting around in the wee hours after the show with the door wide open, sipping our cocktails.

We spotted a group of people walking through the parking lot, and Mr. Guitar-man walked over to the open door in his boxers and watched them. I told him to extend his arm and point at them, and when he did, I started shouting, "Hey, you! You, down there! Get out of my parking lot!"

When the group of people looked up, they stood watching a man in his underwear with the door wide open, shouting and pointing at them. It was hilarious. He just stood there, pointing and laughing.

The following night, we had a show in New Orleans. We figured we'd leave the hotel at 8 a.m. and have plenty of time to make it to Louisiana for the next gig. I don't know what happened, but it took all day just to get out of Florida.

We made it to our hotel as the sun was going down, and had just enough time to get ready and go to the club for a sound check.

As we hung out backstage, waiting for hours until showtime, I decided to grab a beer and go outside and watch the nightlife.

As I was leaning on the wall, sipping my beer, I watched a group of punk rockers exit their vehicle and begin to walk inside the club. I was standing about twenty feet away when one of them looked at me and took a double-take before telling his friends, "Hey, look! It's Beast!"

They walked over to me with smiley faces and kept calling me a beast.

I finished my beer and replied, "You guys want trouble?"

At that moment, our drummer Mark comes out the door and whispers in my ear, "Your name is Bruce Beast, remember?"

Nope, I sure didn't. I forgot all about our stage names from over twenty years ago. There have been so many different players in F since then. Nobody had stage names in F anymore except for Flash and, apparently, me.

After the show, we made it back to our fancy hotel on the water. This hotel was the tallest hotel building on the water. To get the elevator in the lobby to work, you had to enter your hotel number and a combination of other things that I had no access to.

We took our showers and tried to relax. Since I was in New Orleans, I wasn't about to relax. I asked if anybody wanted to go down Bourbon Street and check out the bars, and Mark was the only one to join me. Since it was so late, we decided to drink one beer in every bar before they closed. I could write another book describing the details, but it would be incriminating.

We staggered out of the last bar as the sun was rising. The hotel was on the water, straight down the street, and we couldn't find it to save our lives. When we gave up looking, we leaned on a building to catch our bearings. I suddenly looked up and spotted the hotel—we were leaning on it.

We laughed hysterically and entered the lobby to go to our rooms. We had no clue what the hotel room number was or how to operate the elevators. Somehow, some concerned citizens and hotel staff were kind enough to figure it out and drop us off at the room we were looking for. It was a night to remember.

There were more funny things that happened with this F-lineup, but I won't write them in this book. Too bad Flash and the guitar-man didn't go barhopping with us, or maybe it was for the best. We would probably have wound up in jail.

I understood why Flash couldn't go along; his girlfriend was with him, simple as that. Guitar Man was just plain out of it. He was a funny guy, and I regret forgetting his name. He was sorely missed, as he also joined the group of rockers who left the planet too early.

F was a featured act at a punk-rock festival in Brandon, Florida. The festival took place in a small room with no stage. The crowd was pressed up with the band, and I couldn't hear anything but what sounded like a jet crashing.

Where I would usually watch the guitar player to see what he was playing, this time, I couldn't even see him. I knew I flubbed up the ending of one song, and it pissed me off. I knew Flash wasn't happy.

Another bad show was in Miami at Churchill's. We played with a punk band, The Crumbs, and the sound was horrible. Everything was running late, and we had no soundcheck. Thankfully, our set was cut to 5 songs. I don't know what the guitar player was playing, but it sounded like a tornado tearing through a trailer park.

After four years of debauchery with this lineup of F, drummer Mark quit the band. Since Rob F's newest guitar player lived on the

West Coast, Flash planned to have rehearsals over there, which I had no intention of doing.

Next thing I know, F is regrouped and playing with a new drummer and bass player.

One of the reasons I wasn't willing to go to the West Coast to rehearse was the fact that I was now on the verge of turning 50 years old, and it wasn't convenient for me anymore. It's one thing to be a 50-year-old rock star still playing and selling out stadiums, but I think it's just plain ridiculous for a struggling musician to be up on stage still trying to make it. To me, if there's no light at the end of the tunnel, jump off the train.

Luckily, during my time playing with F, my son dared me to write a book. That was it. The challenge was accepted. I suddenly had more fun trying to write a book than playing music, and the kicker was, it's only me. It was up to me if I finished a book and got it published. I didn't have to worry about a band member not showing up or being cranky…It's just me, and I'm having a blast.

In November 2012, my first book, called 'What Lurks Below' was released through a Pennsylvania publisher, and that was it! I decided to spend the next half of my life being a published author. So far, it's working, but as I sit here writing this book, I still feel the hunger pangs to perform in front of a live audience.

Like the Rolling Stones said, you can't always get what you want, but if you try sometimes, you get what you need.

Right now, I need to get this book and many more published before I exit stage left.

Gone Solo

Easy Access

Back in F!

Playing with Nicko at the same event '05

Easy Access

Easy Access

Easy Access

www.ingramcontent.com/pod-product-compliance
Lightning Source LLC
Chambersburg PA
CBHW021639120626
46545CB00002B/628